A Light Revealing

*The Methodist Episcopal Church
in Early America*

Sharon Grimes Knox

ISBN 978-1-63903-897-8 (paperback)
ISBN 978-1-63903-898-5 (digital)

Copyright © 2021 by Sharon Grimes Knox

All rights reserved. No part of this publication may be reproduced, distributed, or transmitted in any form or by any means, including photocopying, recording, or other electronic or mechanical methods without the prior written permission of the publisher. For permission requests, solicit the publisher via the address below.

Christian Faith Publishing, Inc.
832 Park Avenue
Meadville, PA 16335
www.christianfaithpublishing.com

Printed in the United States of America

For my two lights, John Harlin Grimes Jr. and William Scott Grimes

Preface

In 2004, I came across a well-worn, leather-bound copy of sermons viewed by readers for almost 150 years. Delivered in 1873 and afterwards, these sermons of Rev. James T. Galford inspired me to find out more about the origins of the Methodist Episcopal Church and how this religion spread.

The role of the circuit riders was profound, not only in gaining converts but also in shaping American cultural history. This led me to delving further in the history of the early settlers and how they embraced this new religious discipline.

By the end of the nineteenth century, the Methodist doctrine outpaced all other denominations. Between 1770 and 1820, members grew from fewer than 1,000 to more than 250,000 and, by 1830, nearly half a million. By mid-nineteenth century, American Methodism was almost half again as large as any other Protestant body.[1] The initial thought is, how did this happen? How did they prosper in the trail of the Congregationalists, Presbyterians, and others? The answer is largely to be found in the exuberance of the early circuit riders. Much of the success of this early growth of the Methodists was due to their diligence and the discipline that they instituted. Without the weekly meetings and the growth of the Sunday school, the movement would never have flourished.

This work begins with the Methodist movement in England and the American experiment and its fruition as a homegrown phenomenon. It examines the circuit riders and their extraordinary expe-

---

[1] John H. Wigger, *Taking Heaven by Storm: Methodism and the Rise of Popular Christianity in America*. Urbana and Chicago: University of Illinois Press, (2001), p. 3.

riences while spreading the good news of the Gospel. The Sunday school movement has long been a subject of interest and debate. Was it really a creation of Robert Raikes in England, considered to be its "founder"? How did this movement evolve and adapt to the circumstances in nascent America?

Methodism evolved from the log cabin and camp meetings into an institution both in organization and structure. As small stations grew in response to railway expansion, community spirit evolved. Churches became a source of pride, as did the creation of schools.

Methodism matured through two wars: slavery and division. The creation of conferences and a centralized doctrine played an important part. But it was not until 1968 that the United Methodist Church emerged.

Finally, James T. Galford's sermons attest to a rigid view of religion as a disciplinary necessity. He was a man much in tune with his congregation. Unlike the early circuit riders, he obtained a college education and was a well-respected member of his community. His congregation could identify with his industry in farming and ranching, and he spoke to his congregation with enthusiasm and zeal.

I would like to thank the many librarians and archivists who have assisted me and aided immensely in my research. The staff at the Duke Divinity School Library guided me through the early stages of my research. Anne Marie Boyd, senior library assistant, was particularly helpful in navigating me through many searches. While at Duke, I met with the Rev. Will Willimon, who offered invaluable advice.

In Illinois, I visited several archives and historical associations to gain further knowledge of frontier communities and the growth of the church and the Sunday school movement in the 1800s.

I am deeply indebted to the Lincoln Historical and Genealogical Society and, in particular, Gary Freese. His enthusiasm added to the material that I found on Springbank Methodist Episcopal Church and the Rev. J.T. Galford, its rector. His place in the farming culture of the area is crucial in understanding the role of a circuit rider and his congregation at Springbank.

Tom McLaughlin, director of the Lincoln Heritage Museum, took the time to show me the campus and guide me to the administrative offices. Lincoln College alumni office answered many questions about J.T. Galford. The registrar's office provided important information as to the date of his graduation and his chosen field of study.

In visiting the Great Rivers Conference archives in MacMurray College in Jacksonville, Illinois, I found valuable information about the growth of the conference system and its importance. My thanks to Lauretta Scheller for her assistance and her referral to the Illinois State Archives. I was able to confirm many dates and events in secondary source material.

My sincere thanks to Valerie Casselton, managing editor of the *Vancouver Sun* and *The Province*. Valerie found the time to do a brilliant review of the manuscript and made many helpful suggestions.

Finally, I am indebted to the many anonymous people who preserve the riches of the past. A leather-bound manuscript could just as easily have found its way to a charity shop or a secondhand bookstore. What a waste it would have been not to share Reverend Galford's powerful message.

Chapter 1

Unto thee, O Lord, do I lift up my soul.
—Psalm 25:1

Christ is Made the Sure Foundation.[2]

John Wesley inspired a movement and its adherents. Much is known about this founder of Methodism. He looked to reform the established church in England but created a movement that would have repercussions both at home and abroad.

Wesley was born on June 17, 1703, either the thirteenth or fourteenth child born to Susannah and Samuel Wesley, the rector of Epworth Church in Lincolnshire. Wesley was the seventh child to survive his first year, one daughter and five sons having predeceased him.[3] The question of a middle name for John is also a conundrum. As a matter of record, there is no reference to a middle name.

Although John had used the name "Benjamin" once, the tradition owes more to historians who have perpetuated the fable. What we do know is the entry in the parish records naming him "John Wesley," was written by his father in his own hand.[4] The tradition in the family was to give a child a middle name if he or she survived. In 1699, Susannah had given birth to twin boys—John and Benjamin. Eighteen months before John's birth, a second set of twins was born

---

[2] Text: 7th C. Latin, *Angularis fundamentum*, tr. John Mason Neal (1818–1866). Music: Henry Purcell (1659–1695), adapt. *The Psalmist*, 1842.
[3] The Wesley family were not quite certain of the number of children in total.
[4] Richard P. Heitzenrater, *The Elusive Mr. Wesley*. Nashville: Abingdon Press (2003), pp. 41–42.

and named Anne and John Benjamin. It was not uncommon in the eighteenth century to reuse a name in the case of a deceased infant. As many names were given to honor an adult relative, as well the dead child, it must have been a responsibility.

Two incidents marked Wesley's childhood and had an everlasting effect on his reputation and credibility. The first was a fire in the rectory. His sister, Hetty, woke to fire ashes dropping on her feet. She roused the other children and fled. When all were gathered outside, it became apparent that John was missing.

Any rescue on the part of his parents was futile, beaten back by the flames' intensity and fuelled by a bitter cold night. When John woke up, he saw the flames on his bedroom ceiling. He attempted to open the bedroom door but realized it would be impossible, the floor outside glowing. He climbed on a chest near the window and shouted for help. A more robust man held a lighter fellow on his shoulders, and John climbed down to safety. The rector offered a prayer of thanksgiving for his eight children's safety. That John's rescue foreshadowed a sign of his future as a leader of Christian revival belongs more to Methodist folklore than fact. Only two years later did his mother arrive at the belief that John had been chosen to do God's work. She promised God that she would be "more particularly careful of the soul of this child, that Thou hast so mercifully provided for, then ever I have been."[5]

The second incident happened in the Epworth Rectory, with "disturbances" occurring in 1716–1717. When John was at Oxford, he heard of several incidents where Old Jeffrey visited the rectory. Supposedly, he was a former occupant of the rectory who had committed suicide. He first appeared in the rectory to a parlor maid. The Wesley women thought that she possessed a vivid but childish imagination. But several days later, the women also became aware of Old Jeffrey's presence. Emily asked her mother to come to the nursery which had not been in use for some time. A rocking cradle noise started, accompanied by other competing sounds. Susannah was convinced of his presence yet had no desire to enlighten her

---

[5] Heitzenrater, *Elusive Wesley*, p. 44.

husband at first. But as the incidents occurred frequently, Suky, then twenty-one, informed her father and was chastised for being so credulous. Yet Samuel became conscious of Old Jeffrey's presence when the specter began to knock during the evening prayers. This continued for some time and interfered with both morning and evening prayers, especially those for King William.[6]

The significance of these two events, the fire and the presence of Old Jeffrey, add to the Wesleyan folklore tradition. One reinforces the idea that Wesley was recognized early on as being special, a "brand plucked out from the burning."[7] Yet Wesley refuted this statement: "Indeed not I; I never said so. I am guiltless in this matter."[8]

The Old Jeffrey legend also adds to the image of Wesley as a man in touch with the people. Many in eighteenth-century England fully believed in omens and the supernatural. But the Age of Reason has not yet reached many of the working class who attended Wesley's outdoor meetings. He bridged the gap from being an Oxford-educated scholar and a common man, riding roughly four thousand miles yearly and speaking outdoors to all who would listen. Wesley's methods would find fertile territory in the New World, and his techniques would be adopted by the early circuit riders.

Wesley's formal education began at Charterhouse, one of the preeminent public schools in England. He entered as a foundation scholar or "gown boy" at the age of thirteen and left with a thorough knowledge of Latin and Greek. In June 1720, he was elected as an exhibitioner of Christ Church, Oxford. His exhibitions from Charterhouse and Christ Church amounted to forty pounds a year.

Although he enjoyed the usual collegiate entertainments in the beginning, he was conscious of their cost both to his income as well as his spiritual state. The early years at Christ Church are full of introspection and self-doubt. His diary entries consist of various lists of questions which led him to examine himself daily and sometimes hourly.[9]

---

[6] Ibid., pp. 46–51.
[7] Amos 4:11, Zech. 3:2.
[8] Heitzenrater, *Elusive Wesley*, p. 45.
[9] Ibid., pp. 59–62.

Wesley was elected a fellow of Lincoln College, in Oxford, in 1726. He received his master's degree in 1727 and, having been ordained a deacon in 1725, became an Anglican priest in 1728. He spent time preaching in churches in London and throughout England and Ireland. He also served as a curate for his father and as an assistant pastor at Wroot, Lincolnshire.

In 1729, he returned to Oxford. "It was my full resolve to live and die there."[10] In these years, a club was formed. The group consisted of John, Wesley's brother, Charles, William, and one or two others who were eager to examine the tenets of Christian living and adopt them. Initially, they met three or four times a week to discuss the classics and often religious works on Sunday.

But the Holy Club, as it was known, quickly became more than just another Oxford social club. The idea that self-examination was essential was coupled with the expectation that others were expected to do the same. But it was the lists and questions about what comprised the Christian life that led them to be deemed Methodists. Other less flattering names for members of the Holy Club were: Bible Moths, Supererogation Men, the Godly Men, Sacramentarians, and Enthusiasts.[11]

Another distinct feature of the Holy Club men was their adherence to the belief that the quest for holiness and good works were not incompatible. In the eighteenth century, few people or organizations devoted themselves to care for the poor. The Holy Club's sentiment laid the roots for the Victorian era. Institutions such as the Salvation Army, Doctor Barnardo's, the RSPCA, and the Royal National Institute for the Blind are just a few examples of the developing national social conscience.

Wesley and other members of the Holy Club were eager to engage in active work in prisons and among the poor. He wrote to his father for endorsement of his plans which met with approval. Samuel Wesley himself had experience of prison work as an undergradu-

---

[10] Ibid., p. 45.
[11] Roy Hattersley, *John Wesley: A Brand from the Burning*. London, Abacus (2004), p. 73.

ate. At the father's suggestion, Wesley met with a prison chaplain who asked the local bishop's approval and the work began. Before long, the members extended their work to include visiting the poor. William Morgan, a fellow member, formed a "ragged school for the children of the Oxford slums." When he became too ill to continue in the university, the Holy Club raised the funds to hire a substitute for the school.[12]

In engaging in charitable works, the Holy Club raised the argument: is assurance a product of faith alone, or do good works lead to salvation? This would be a question that Wesley would wrestle with for much of his life.

The year 1735 ushered in two events that tested Wesley and his faith: the death of his father, Samuel, and the possibility of returning to Epworth and the ministry there. While considering this position, his father died but not before Wesley made a defense of his decision to remain in Oxford. "I cannot quit my first conclusion that I am not likely to do that good anywhere, not even Epworth, which I may do in Oxford."[13]

The second event had to do with John Oglethorpe, member of Parliament and philanthropist. As founder of the colony of Georgia in British America, he hoped to resettle deserving poor who were jailed as debtors. Interested early in prison reform, he set up a committee to study prison conditions. The Committee of Inquiry into Debtors' Gaols was introduced into the House of Commons. It would take years to gain success. As late as 1970, a person could be jailed for debt.[14]

---

[12] Hattersley, *Brand*, p. 78 and Richard P. Heitzenrater, *Elusive Wesley*, pp. 69–71. William Morgan died on August 26, 1732. His father, Richard Morgan, largely blamed Methodism and Wesley in particular for his demise by adding fasting to the club's beliefs. Wesley outlined the beliefs of Oxford Methodist practices in his defense. His success found Richard Morgan's second son, Richard Jr., under Wesley's care.

[13] Heitzenrater, *Elusive Wesley*, p. 72.

[14] As late as the 1970s, it was still possible for a person to go to Debtors' Prison, but they were incarcerated in regular, low-offense prisons. The term "Debtors' Prison" referred by then to the nature of the crime. One could be convicted if council taxes had not been paid for three months.

Oglethorpe did not give up. He criticized the fact that many debtors could not leave prison to work. Therefore, it was a vicious cycle as if they could not work, they could not make the necessary money to pay off their debts.

Oglethorpe was given lands in Georgia, largely recognized by the House of Commons as a barrier to Spanish (and Catholic) encroachment. Oglethorpe sought to make a settlement in Georgia and transported some debtors to work there. More than anything, Georgia was to be a Christian settlement and a moral one.

Influenced by Oglethorpe, Wesley left for Georgia onboard the ship Simmonds with the intention of preaching to the American Indians. Instead, he found himself appointed pastor in Savannah. He approached the position in a zealous manner, which won him advocates among his faithful parishioners but also critics. One of his positive contributions was the founding of a small society which met in his home following evening prayer.

Those who criticized saw the society as an intrusion into private lives and matters. Wesley firmly stated his objective in creating this society. The meeting's purpose was to "reprove, instruct and exhort one another."[15]

Wesley considered returning to England. "Neither had I found or heard of yet any Indians on the continent of America who had the least desire of being instructed." Previous attempts by the Spanish to convert the Indians ended in suspicion concerning the missionaries' intentions. While initially still aboard the *Simmonds*, the Indians, Tomo-Chachi, his nephew Thleeanouhee, his wife Sinuarky, and others, came onboard to express their welcome. Tomo-Chachi added a caveat: "But we would not be made Christians as the Spanish make Christians: we would be taught, before we are baptized."[16] The Spanish had killed Tomo-Chachi's own father for refusing to be baptized. The welcoming party arranged a meeting with other Indians in a village where John and Charles Wesley were to make camp. When

---

[15] Percy Livingstone Parker, ed., *The Journal of John Wesley: Founder of the Methodist Movement*. N.P., F.H. Revell (2016), p. 34.
[16] Ibid., p. 32.

they arrived there, the village was deserted.[17] Perhaps, this was a foreshadowing of their tenuous relationship to come.

Remaining in Savannah, Wesley developed a relationship with one of his female parishioners, Sophia Christina Hopkey, the niece of the chief magistrate, Thomas Causton. Sophia, not yet eighteen, was fifteen years younger than Wesley. The attraction that evolved was mutual.

However, this was not the first time that Wesley's romantic intentions caused concern. He had an experience while in the Cotswolds in 1726, meeting sisters Betty Kirkham and Sarah (Sally) Kirkham Chapone. Sally might have been a married woman, but her affection for Wesley was undeniable. Wesley records in his diary: "Sat with Varanese [Sally] and Betty till eleven. Leaned on Varanese's breast and kept both her hands within mine."[18] As was the custom in the eighteenth century, many adopted classical names which were used in their more intimate social circles. Wesley would wrestle with his desire for intimacy, despite seeing celibacy as "the more excellent way."[19] Wesley did not marry until he was forty in 1751. The marriage to Mary Vazeille was an unhappy one, and all attempts at reconciliation ended in 1771.

Initially, Sophia and John's relationship was spiritual, meeting frequently after public prayers in the mornings and evenings. But Wesley records many chances of temptation to expand their relationship. In addition to instructing Sophy in religious matters, he introduced French which they studied daily. They were forced to sit close to each other. "My greatest difficulty was, while I was teaching her French when being obliged (as having but one book) to sit close to her, unless I prayed without ceasing, I could not avoid using some familiarity or other which was not needful. Sometimes, I put my arm around her waist, sometimes took her by the hand, and sometimes kissed her."[20]

---

[17] Hattersley, *Brand*, p. 111.
[18] Heitzenrater, *Elusive Wesley*, p. 56.
[19] Ibid, p. 77.
[20] Heitzenrater, *Elusive Wesley*, p. 80.

As their friendship developed, Wesley remained conflicted. It became clear that as John wrestled with the decision between marriage and celibacy, Sophy grew increasingly impatient with the reluctant suitor. On March 9, on Sophy's request, Mrs. Causton asked Wesley to publish the banns of marriage between her and William Williamson, a clerk in her uncle's store. But if this was a bid to force Wesley to make a decision for marriage, it was unsuccessful. On March 12, 1737, Sophy became Mrs. Williamson, in a marriage without the necessary banns, in Purrysburg, South Carolina.

Wesley then warned Sophy that she had failed her need to repent her sins before taking communion. When she did not comply, Wesley banned her from communion.[21] The following day, Wesley received a warrant to answer the Williamsons' complaint of defamation. The indictment listed ten total complaints touching every complaint made since he arrived in Savannah.

Despite numerous appearances, the court was not satisfied.[22] Wesley resolved to flee, despite a visit from Causton and others forbidding him to leave. On December 2, 1737, he left for Carolina and boarded the ship *Samuel* for the voyage back to England. He expressed his lack of success as "It is now two years and four months since I left my native country in order to teach the Georgia Indians the nature of Christianity. But what have I found myself in the meantime? Why least of all what I expected, that I, who went to America to convert the Indians, was never myself converted to God."[23]

On return, Wesley entered a period of intense self-examination unlike any previous attempts. During the initial voyage to Georgia aboard the *Simmonds*, he met a group of Moravians (or as he referred to them, "Germans"). He was impressed by their piety and calmness in the face of danger from the storms they encountered. He noticed, "I had long before observed the great seriousness of their behavior. Of their humility, they had given a continual proof by performing those

---

[21] Hattersley, *Brand*, p. 121.
[22] Heitzenrater, *Elusive Wesley*, pp. 86–89.
[23] Hattersley, *Brand*, p. 125.

servile offices for the other passengers, which none of the English would undertake."[24]

Later, Wesley would spend three months in Germany absorbing much of the Moravian spirit. The pivotal moment in John Wesley's quest for the true meaning of faith began to find fruition in the Aldersgate experience. The Aldersgate Street society met for a reading of Martin Luther's Epistle to the Romans. "While he was describing the change which God works in the heart through faith in Christ, I felt my heart strangely warmed. I felt I did trust in Christ, Christ alone, for salvation; and assurance was given me that He had taken away my sins, even mine, and saved me from the law of sin and death."[25] This assurance was not to be everlasting, and John Wesley would spend a lifetime wrestling with the concepts of prevenient grace, assurance of pardon for sins, and sanctification.[26] These tenets would be both a personal and universal quest.

John Wesley was not a systematic theologian but a man of extraordinary vitality, a man who could travel by horseback and deliver over forty thousand sermons in his lifetime. It was his gift to touch the common person, the miner, the farmer, and others who lived ordinary lives. He left a legacy for the hard-riding, religious pioneers who followed.

---

[24] Parker, ed., *Journal*, p. 31.
[25] Parker, ed., *Journal*, pp. 56–57.
[26] Prevenient meaning God's grace coming before a belief in Christ.

Chapter 2

Whom shall I send and who will go for us?
—Isaiah 6:8

Tell out my soul, the greatness of the Lord.

The success of Methodism is, in large part, due to the zeal of the first itinerant preachers. They went forth to spread the Gospel in uncertain times with a conviction that was unparalleled. But it was their zeal and their ability to reach the common folk that set them apart from other denominations. They identified with itinerants who spoke the vernacular and who shared a similar background. Largely artisan, unschooled, but committed, these itinerants forged a common bond: the love of Christ.[27]

Itinerant preachers in America represented a distinct social class, largely from the same class as their audiences: artisan and the middling sort. Unlike their counterparts, the college-educated Presbyterians, Congregationalists, and Episcopalians, they spoke in familiar terms to their audiences. As theologian C.S. Lewis later asserted, "The vernacular is the real test. If you can't turn your faith into it, then either you don't understand it or you don't believe it."[28]

Charles Giles, an itinerant himself, related an incident in Connecticut of "certain religionists" whom many saw as "irregular and unauthorized." Was this truly a new sect? Possibly Methodists?

---

[27] John H. Wigger, *Taking Heaven by Storm: Methodism and the Rise of Popular Christianity in America*. Urbana and Chicago: University of Illinois Press (2001), p. 48.

[28] Ibid., pp. 48–49.

He comments on the lack of literacy of two Methodist preachers looking to find lost sinners during his boyhood in Connecticut: "The fact that they were illiterate men, possessing only a common share of native talent, made the work appear more strange and marvelous."[29]

Giles made the connection between the itinerant and the common man. Higher education while laudable did not prevent the often-unlettered itinerant from reaching the heart of the these people. "It is admitted, that profound learning has ever been, and ever will be, an important acquisition for the minister of the gospel; to enable him to expound the Christian religion, and to meet the subtle arguments of the caviling world. Still, God will have ministers, and, if holy learned men are not at hand, he *can* take, and *will* take, men of unpolished, unlettered minds, that glow with a pious flame, and send them out, under divine influences, to proclaim the great salvation."[30]

Francis Asbury, later to become a bishop, worked as a blacksmith. His appointment as a preacher was typical for a Methodist itinerant: only one year on any given circuit. Contrast this with the New England clergy where a lifetime commitment to a single congregation was the norm.

Conversion became a common occurrence at meetings or in dreams. It "laid the foundation for a deep sense of personal piety."[31] After a series of vivid dreams, Benjamin Abbott, a hatter's apprentice and later a farmer, was profoundly moved. "The word reached my heart in such a powerful manner that it shook every joint in my body. Tears flowed in abundance and I cried out for mercy."[32]

Travel by the early circuit riders was arduous. Freeborn Garrettson claimed he had traveled over 100,000 miles between 1776 and 1793. The itinerant life has often been described as solitary. Yet the close fellowship that developed among them challenges

---

[29] Charles Giles, *Pioneer: A Narrative of the Nativity, Experience, Travels. And Ministerial Labours of Rev. Charles Giles*. New York: G. Lane and P.P. Sandford (1844), p. 259.
[30] Giles, *Pioneer*, p. 61.
[31] Wigger, *Taking Heaven*, p. 54.
[32] 32. Ibid.

this belief. Letter writing was the glue that bound the "band of brothers" together. Also many made long-lasting friendship through other means. Attendance at organized Methodist meetings brought them closer to each other.[33] The brothers shared many challenging problems: familial opposition, lodging conditions, violence, and the quandary of choosing marriage or celibacy concerned them all.

Familial opposition became a major concern for many. Dan Young's mother pleaded with him to join the Presbyterians or Baptists—not Methodists. John Cooper's father threw a "shovelful of hot embers" on his son when he found him praying. Even the itinerant himself, after censure by a parent, had doubts. Billy Hibbard commented, "I wanted to be a Congregationalist and to be respectable. But I wanted the love and seriousness of the Methodists." Hibbard faced his own opposition. His wife was embarrassed by his early public speaking, and his father threatened to disinherit him. His father "reproved me for preaching, because I had not been educated in college."[34]

Most itinerants did not have the funds to pay for lodging, often staying in the homes where they preached. Thomas Smith might have anticipated bedbugs and fleas, but there were other surprises. He was shown the room where a man had died that morning. He did not last the night, finding a tree root outside to finish his sleep.[35] On another occasion, Henry Smith lodged in a house with only one bed. When it was time to go to sleep, the woman placed the bed before the fire and asked Smith to lie down on one end "and it answered very well for me, the man and his wife, and two children."[36]

The weather played no small part in the itinerant's lodging. Travelling with her itinerant-preacher husband, Mary Tucker spent a blustering night in a bedroom with holes in the walls and the roof so large that she awoke in ankle-deep snow.[37]

---

[33] Ibid., p. 62.
[34] Ibid, p. 58.
[35] Ibid, p. 60.
[36] Henry Smith, *Recollections*, p. 22.
[37] Wigger, *Taking Heaven*, p. 69.

Itinerants recognized the harsh conditions people faced. Toward the end of his career, Henry Smith said he had conquered any prejudices he had about eating, drinking, or lodging. "I could submit to any kind of inconvenience when I had an opportunity of doing good. My call was among the poor, and among them, I could feel myself at home."[38] Speaking at Clarksburg, he said, "They were all backwoods people, and came to the meeting in backwoods style—all on foot; a considerable congregation. I looked round and saw one old man who had shoes on his feet. The preacher wore Indian moccasins; every man, woman, and child besides, was barefooted."

Although there was a preacher present, as circuit preacher, Henry Smith delivered the sermon: "I did my best, and soon found if there were no shoes and fine dresses in the congregation, there were attentive hearers, and feeling hearts; for the melting power of the Lord came down upon us, and we felt that the great Head of the church was in the midst of us. In meeting the class, I heard the same humble, loving, religious experience, that I had often heard in better-dressed societies. If this scene did not make a backwoodsman of me outright, it at least reconciled me to the people, and I felt happy among them."[39]

Danger was ever present, coming both from nature and man. Henry Smith describes a remedy for a rattlesnake bite he learned from Old Brother Hacker: "Why I had a handful of salt in my pocket; I spit some tobacco juice among it, and tied it on with my handkerchief and walked home."[40] Smith himself recalled crushing the head of a rattlesnake.

Riding the circuit was full of risks in an unknown land. Trails were often unmarked, and the challenges of crossing streams and rivers posed particular problems. Lack of trails meant Henry Smith needed a boat to cross the Ohio River. Waiting until the water rose and a boat arrived, Smith joined two families, thirteen horses, and two or three in the families had measles.[41]

---

[38] Henry Smith, *Recollections*, p. 15.
[39] Ibid, p. 14.
[40] 40. Henry Smith, *Recollections*, p. 13.
[41] Ibid., pp. 28–29.

Indians posed a particular problem in that they were familiar with the territory and were skilled hunters. Speaking at Edward West's home, whose first wife had been killed by Indians and her sister, Margaret, scalped, West showed Margaret's head to Smith: "The skin on the crown of the head was all taken off, except a little about the forehead; and a thin white skin had grown over that place but no hair. She appeared to enjoy pretty good health."[42]

The Canadian part of the circuit brought its own challenges. Circuit rider F. Brown related a particularly frightening incident. A panther had come to the logs just over his bed and put his paws on the windowsill, glaring at him. Growling, he turned away, but Brown spent the rest of the night firmly fixed in case his movement caused the panther to lunge and strike.[43]

Itinerant preachers had few possessions to carry. The horse was equipped with a bear skin rug, twin saddlebags, a valise, and the all-important notebook, which held sermon notes, the crude circuit map, a Bible, journals, and an accounting of the books sold of the Methodist Book Concern.[44] Often, he had to make a choice between additional books or personal items.

Clothing was necessary but limited, and the rough terrain, fording streams and rivers, and travelling by horseback took its toll. Henry Smith observed: "Most of my clothes by this time had become threadbare and some worn out, and I had no money to buy new ones." On one occasion he had to sleep in his overcoat to hide the "rents in my clothes."[45]

James Jenkins itinerated for fifteen years and kept a diary of his salary. He received $22, $64, $54, $64, $64, $64, $64, $64, $64, $80, $160, and $140 per annum.[46] James Quinn itinerated for forty years and computed that the church owed him some $2,600 in

---

[42] Ibid, pp. 16–17.
[43] Rev. James Erwin, *Recollections of Early Circuit Life*. Toledo, Ohio: Spear, Johnson & Coe, Printers (1884), p. 297.
[44] Peter Feinman, *Itinerant Circuit-riding Minister: Warrior of Light in a Wilderness of Chaos*. Methodist History; 45:1 (October 2006).
[45] Henry Smith, *Recollections*, pp. 21–22.
[46] Wigger, *Taking Heaven*, p. 61.

unpaid salary and expenses.[47] Only belief and dedication were at the root of itineracy.

The zeal displayed by the early circuit riders, and its effectiveness is remarkable. But there can be no doubt that their presence was not welcomed by all. Because they were not fixed in a particular location, they often were resisted by the local clergy. Often, the established clergy tried to limit this "invading army" by attempting to forbid them to preach in their territory and denying them communion.[48] Wesley comments, "God in Scripture commands me, according to my power to instruct the ignorant, reform the wicked, confirm the virtuous. Man forbids me to do this in another's parish. Whom then shall I hear, God or man? I look upon all the world as my parish."[49]

Clergy were not the only ones to resent the zealous preachers whom they regarded as intruders. One family had not even unpacked their wagon before Richard Nolley found them. The father exclaimed, "What have you found me already? Another Methodist preacher!" The man had left Virginia and Georgia, hoping to break the Methodists' hold on his wife and daughter.[50]

Other itinerants met with violence. Freeborn Garrettson was beaten, was close to being shot and hanged before being thrown into jail. But equally dramatic was the incident he had with one family. He arrived at their home, tired and thirsty. The woman of the house went to get him something to drink and returned after fifteen minutes with a small beer. Garrettson's suspicions were aroused when he lifted the cup but put it down immediately. When dinner was served, he ate little. The next morning, Garrettson found that she had poisoned her husband and two others with the meat intended for him. The woman remarked that she would put an end to the Methodists.[51]

To marry or remain celibate was a difficult choice. The band of brothers' close connection was challenged by a growing tendency to

---

[47] Ibid.
[48] Abel Stevens, *History of the Methodist Episcopal Church in the United States of America* (New York: Eaton and Mains [1900]), 1:38, as quoted in Feinman, p. 44.
[49] Feinman, *Circuit*, pp. 44–45.
[50] 50. Wigger, *Taking Heaven*, p. 56.
[51] Stevens, History, Vol. 2, Part 28, p. 31.

marry. Celibacy was a necessary norm among itinerants who rode the circuit in the early years, when one considered the expense of travelling with a wife and children. But the concept of itinerant preaching and the preachers' expectations changed by the middle of the nineteenth century.

In some situations, wives traveled with their preacher husbands. Henry Smith recalls meeting a couple in Kentucky. Each had a horse equipped with a saddle and saddlebags and traveled the circuit with their possessions intact.[52]

Henry Smith voiced an opinion on married clergy, "Better take one well made, well married, laborious, enterprising minister of Jesus Christ, than half a dozen such fickle-minded boys."[53]

Despite all the obstacles, why did the early itinerants succeed? Perhaps because they spoke in backwoods style and were in tune with their listeners. The structure of early Methodism through class meetings, camp, and quarterly meetings allowed for self-examination and the opportunity for religious enthusiasm. Equally important was the concept of a shared experience in the quest for religious meaning in their rural and often isolated lives.

In the itinerant, people had a preacher who understood adversity and shared challenges. It was this connection in faith and frontier challenges that made Methodism a force in American culture and civilization.

---

[52] Henry Smith, *Recollections*, p. 26.
[53] Wigger, *Taking Heaven*, p. 68.

Chapter 3

Suffer the little children to come unto me.
—Mark 10:14

Jesus wants me for a sunbeam.[54]

Religious education for children took on a new vitality with the work of Robert Raikes (1736–1811). Raikes was a successful newspaper publisher in Gloucester, England. Embracing the Humanitarian movement with his interest in prison reform, he identified a connection between ignorance and poverty and vice. Education, knowledge, and enlightenment should produce the opposite of vice—namely goodness, morality, and righteousness.[55]

Initially, Raikes focused on the prisoners themselves, paying for an educated debtor in prison to teach fellow prisoners to read. Finding little success, he realized that adults were often set on a course of habits that was well established. Education must begin with the child.

The factory child in the eighteenth century led a dismal life. Most adults and children in Gloucester worked in pin making. Adam Smith, in his *Inquiry into the Nature and Causes of the Wealth of Nations*, describes the tediousness of pin manufacturing. Working six days a week, Sunday was the factory child's one day of freedom. Parents often paid little attention to their children as they pursued

---

[54] Text: Nellie Talbert, Music: E.O. Excell
[55] Chris Clarke, *"Robert Raikes and the Sunday School Movement,"* An address given to Crich Baptist Church, Crich, Derbyshire, England. April 25, 2015, p. 5.

their own pleasures. Dirty ragamuffins roamed the streets of the cathedral city, singing bawdy songs.

Raikes's first attempt in 1780 at organizing these children was to persuade them to meet him in the cathedral yard at 7:00 a.m. His goal was to teach them the catechism, and he failed miserably. One can imagine the impact of a gentleman trying to forge a connection with fifty or so children who had little interest in learning. William Brick, a former Sunday school scholar, recalled one or two boys arriving with fourteen-pound weights attached to their legs to keep them from running away. He spoke of others: "Sometimes boys would be sent to school with logs of wood tied to their ankles, just as though they were wild jackasses, which I suppose they were, only worse."[56]

The next attempt was more successful. Raikes hired a Mrs. Meredith whom he paid one shilling a week to supervise the school in Sooty Lane, named for the chimney sweeps who lived there. A second school was opened in Southgate Street, and the Sooty Street scholars moved to better surroundings and teachers.[57]

Sunday's schedule was fixed with children arriving at 10:00 a.m. and engaged in lessons until noon. They would return at 1:00 p.m. for more lessons until 4:00 p.m. Then they would attend a short church service in St. Mary de Crypt Church until 5:30 p.m. Within three years, the city of Gloucester demonstrated a remarkable change, with less noise and wild behavior. More schools opened here, and the movement spread elsewhere. By 1811, the year of Raikes's death, some fifty thousand children attended Sunday schools in the British Isles.[58]

Raikes's work was continued by Hannah Moore (1745–1833), a playwright and a member of the Clapham Sect, a group of evangelical Christians who lived near the village of Clapham in south London. The group opposed the slave trade. Their interests were not unilateral: bearbaiting, bullfighting, suspension of the lottery, and

---

[56] J. Henry Harris, Josiah Harris, *Robert Raikes. The Man and His Work*. New York: E.P. Dutton & Company (1899), p. 38.
[57] Clarke, *An Address*, p. 5.
[58] Encyclopedia Britannica, *Sunday School*, Extract, p. 1. This is an entry that is very informative and thorough.

prison improvement were all concerns. These challenges could be met by transforming morals and society.[59]

Accordingly, one of the most visible of the Clapham Society was William Wilberforce, British politician and abolitionist. Tirelessly working to end the evils of slavery, Wilberforce introduced bill after bill in Parliament. Eighteen years after he started his antislavery campaign, Parliament passed the Slavery Abolition Act of 1833, the year of his death.

William Wilberforce encouraged religious societies and became involved in church school education. A firm friend of Hannah Moore, Wilberforce and the Clapham Sect financed Hannah and her sister Martha in the development of Sunday schools.

Sunday schools did not evolve in England alone but on the continent and in the colonies. John Wesley recognized the importance of religious education, not only for its present value but also for the future. He brought the concept of Sunday schools to Savannah while he was serving as a missionary. He regularly met with thirty or forty children to catechize them before the evening church service. And as late as April 1788, he writes in his journal: "About three I met between nine hundred and a thousand of the children belonging to our Sunday schools. I never saw such a sight before. They all were exactly clean, as well as plain, in their apparel. All were serious and well behaved."[60]

Wesley held firm beliefs concerning education. He had a clear plan, as he outlined in 1749: "We design to train up children there, if God permits, in every branch of useful learning...till they are fit as to all the acquired qualification for the work of the ministry."[61] Wesley's plan was ambitious. He both wrote the curriculum and composed the texts to be used. As indicative of his own broad education, he included many classics. The first year students read Latin, Greek, Hebrew, and French grammar in preparation for future study.

---

[59] The Moody Church History Timeline, *The Clapham Group*. Christianity.com. (Salem Web Network): 2016, p. 2.
[60] Parker, ed., *Journal*, p. 361.
[61] Hattersley, *Brand*, p. 220.

The second year's curriculum puzzled a few. In addition to classics such as Augustine's *Confessions*, Euclid's *Elements*, and Homer's *Odyssey*, he included Spenser's *The Faerie Queene*. While some favored an expurgated version, Wesley believed the poem to be a moral and religious poem,[62] worthy of inclusion.

The third and fourth years focused on the classics, including Livy, Tacitus, Shakespeare, and other eclectic subjects. In concluding his method, Wesley observes: "Whoever carefully goes through this course will be a better scholar than nine in ten of the graduates at Oxford or Cambridge."[63]

The influence of Robert Raikes and John Wesley on American Sunday school development is undeniable. Each believed in a moral purpose to education. Each recognized the necessity for secular studies. It became more than just learning the three Rs. But there were many problems to be solved. The itinerant might attempt to hold informal studies for the children in his circuit, but he was often riding four hundred to five hundred miles in a four-week circuit.[64] There could be little continuity in childhood religious education.

Missionaries were encouraged to travel the new lands and provide education for those children of parents who were unable to afford private schooling. The teachers were handicapped by a lack of unified curriculum since this work was primarily in religious education and competed with the Sunday school's emergence. The separation of mission school and church school did not occur until the 1850s to 1860s.

Perhaps, unsurprisingly, the Sunday school movement did not have a smooth path. The objective was formally stated in 1790 in the *Minutes* of the annual conferences: "What can be done to instruct poor children (white or black) to read? Let us labor, as the heart and soul of one man, to establish Sunday Schools in, or near the place of public worship."[65]

---

[62] Ibid, p. 219.
[63] Ibid. There is some debate as to Wesley's reference including Oxford, his own university. (Some sources quote both and others just Cambridge.)
[64] Wigger, *Taking Heaven*, pp. 58–59.
[65] John Q. Schisler, *Christian Education in Local Methodist Churches*. Nashville and New York: Abington Press (1969), p. 25.

The Sunday school faced the challenge of churches that were resistant to teaching secular subjects in a place consecrated for worship. Those who were more tolerant gave little financial aid or support to the teachers. As tax-supported public schools became more numerous, they absorbed the teaching of secular subjects, and the Sunday schools could concentrate on being the school of religion.[66]

There also was the curriculum question. Bishop Francis Asbury suggested to John Dickens that he prepare a short scripture catechism. Coupled with tracts and the reading of the Bible, Sunday schools made do with these sole educational materials.[67]

It took organizational growth to solve the problems of the early Sunday school. The American Sunday School Union was established in 1824, being more interested in evangelism and the schools as missionary undertakings. Recognizing the need for specifically Methodist Sunday schools, the Sunday School Union of the Methodist Episcopal Church was organized on April 2, 1827, with Dr. Nathan Bangs as its first corresponding secretary.[68] Bangs was quick to recognize the need for publications for teachers and children alike. Publications soon appeared, and the *Child's Magazine* was started.[69] The purpose was somewhat sobering. "It is intended to embrace in this little work short practical essays, anecdotes, narratives, accounts of the conversion and happy deaths of children, facts illustrative of the conduct of Providence, sketches of natural history, poetry, etc." One wonders how a child's death can be seen as happy and set a positive example of Christian life.

Years before the union formed, the Tract Society of America (1824) and the Tract Society of the Methodist Church (1817) appeared. Tracts joined the union's publication and the Bible as the basis of children's instruction in religious literature. Without a coordinated program, the groups were limited. The Sunday School Union was officially recognized by the 1840 General Conference.[70]

---

[66] Ibid, p. 26.
[67] Ibid., p. 27.
[68] Ibid., p. 28.
[69] Ibid., p. 29.
[70] Schisler, *Christian Education*, p. 33.

One of the problems arising in the beginning was the pastor's role in the Sunday school. As seen, there was reluctance if not hostility to opening the church to Sunday schools. As secular education developed along a separate path, relations between the individual church and its Sunday school gradually improved. The teachers were laypeople, and their suitability for overseeing the children's religious education was at times limited. As the commonality of materials for Sunday school instruction grew, so did the quality of teaching methods. By 1846, there was a call for "normal classes for (Sunday school) teachers on the basis of 'Teachers' Institutes' for secular teaching." Churches were urged to provide tools such as a teacher's library and a Bible class for teachers, in addition to a yearly course of lectures.[71]

This promotion of teachers left the relationship with pastors unanswered. Did the pastors have any responsibility to nurture the Sunday school? Did they have any financial responsibility?

These questions were answered in the General Conferences of 1840 and 1869. In 1840, general recognition was given to the Sunday School Union and gave the pastor the duty to form Bible classes for older youth. And in 1846, the conference recognized the need for graded books for differing ages.[72]

That the Sunday school movement in America has been successful is without doubt. Even in its early years, membership grew dramatically. Sunday schools' objective was the conversion of children and their admission to church membership. Teaching the Gospel was the first step.

---

[71] Ibid., p. 54.
[72] Ibid., pp. 33–34.

Chapter 4

Upon this rock I will build my church.
—Matthew 16:18

Christ is made the sure foundation.[73]

John Wesley never intended to start a new religion. He remained faithful to his upbringing as a member of the Church of England. What he did was to create a method which would rejuvenate the Christian and also speak to the hearts of those yet to be converted. At first, the structure of the Methodists seemed loose and unformed. From 1769, preaching circuits, class meetings, and quarterly meetings formed the basic structure with annual conferences being added in 1773. But this nascent organization proved sufficient.

Class meetings initially provided the continuity necessary for the growth of the new emerging religion. Circuit riders identified a small group and chose a leader. The weekly meetings were supervised by this leader, and records of attendance were kept. White tickets were the key to class meeting membership, and members were approved by the circuit preacher and class leader. Attendance rules were strict: three absences in succession either for illness or other good reason negated a person's eligibility.[74] This effectively closed the door to class meetings.

---

[73] Text: Latin, 7th Century, trans. John Mason Neale; Music: Henry Purcell (Westminster Abbey).

[74] Charles W. Ferguson, *Methodists and the Making of America: Organizing to Beat the Devil*. Austin, Texas: Eakin Press (1983), p. 69.

Twelve to fifteen members made up the meeting. After a hymn, prayers, and Scripture were read, the questioning by the leader commenced. The leader would examine one member at a time, ferreting out answers. Some leaders asked specific questions of each member, strong drink being a popular subject. William Cravens, a local preacher, met with two men who wanted to become preachers. Spotting deficiencies, he said that he "would as soon hear a Negro play a banjo or a raccoon squeal as to hear a negro-holder and a petty lawyer preach."[75] Cravens was a large man, some 333 pounds with a powerful voice and one eye, who was considered an eccentric genius.[76] He was not alone in his moral code and the desire to enforce it.

Another prominent feature in the growth of Methodism in America was the camp meeting, a gathering of worshippers meeting out-of-doors for worship and fellowship. Nineteenth-century historians met them with some hesitancy if not hostility. Church leader and editor Nathan Bangs warned readers of camp meetings being either scenes of disorder or wonderful reformations.[77]

The importance of the woodland setting cannot be disputed. The forests, groves, and gardens offered serenity and a time for reflection. Many a conversion occurred in nature, both by laypeople and the itinerants. John Kobler, in 1790, is touched by divinity: "This morning I feel a great hunger and thirst after righteousness. I retired into a wood where I found the Lord to be very precious to my soul." And later, "This morning I retired into the wood, where I had the sweetness in communing with my beloved Savior."[78] Surely, this woodland setting brought comfort and assurance to preachers who faced the difficult challenges of frontier life.

The evolution of the camp meeting occurred by circumstance, an ad hoc solution. Itinerants faced conditions that defied preparation. Without money to stay in an inn, staying in host cabins was

---

[75] Ferguson, *Methodists*, pp. 72–73.
[76] George Brown, *Recollections of Itinerant Life: Including Early Reminiscences.* Cincinnati: Carroll & Co. Publishers (1866), p. 89.
[77] Russell E. Richey, *Methodism in the American Forest.* New York: Oxford University Press (2015), p. 122.
[78] Ibid, p. 40.

the logical choice, if welcomed. Not infrequently, this cabin had only one room. This room also served as a place for church meetings which was quickly outgrown.

Sometimes, the solution to this problem was a public house. Preacher William Wood held a service in a room adjacent to the bar where a poker game was being played. He had to interrupt the game to call one of the players "to pitch a tune" for the congregation.[79] This was not an isolated incident. Saloons, dance halls, and tree stumps were all available choices.[80]

As crowds grew in number, the setting evolved from the tree stump to the woodlands. Even barns became insufficient for their size. An open field was chosen and developed into a place for larger meetings. Initially, they were crude settings, but because the meetings could last between five and seven days, some provisions became necessary. The site could be from two to four acres. The encampment could be in an open horseshoe, oblong or circular design, the latter being the most popular choice. In the interior would be a pulpit at one end or even a second at the other end if there were more than two preachers. The pulpit would be made of fallen logs with a flat board over them. Women sat in the first row of seats, followed by a second row of men. Outside in the first row would be the people's tents, followed by their wagons and then the horses. People soon learned to bring their own provisions.[81]

The camp meetings became the scene for very emotional displays in the heat of religious frenzy. The outbursts took several forms. There was falling, rolling, jerking, running, singing, dancing, laughing, and barking.

Contemporary Barton W. Stone gives an account: "The falling exercise was very common among all classes, the saints and sinners of every age and every grade, from the philosopher to the clown. The subject of this exercise would generally begin with a piercing scream,

---

[79] Charles A. Johnson, *The Frontier Camp: Religion's Harvest Time*. Dallas: Southern Methodist University Press: (1955), p. 24.
[80] Ibid, pp. 41–45.
[81] Ibid, p. 9.

fall like a log on the floor, earth or mud, and appear as dead."[82] The experience might last fifteen minutes or six to ten hours. Jerking was yet another response to enthusiasm. One person might respond differently from the next afflicted. Jerking could affect different parts of the body but perhaps most frequently the head. But it also could occur all over the body or in a specific part. When the head was affected, the person might move backward or forward or from one side to the other in rapid motion. The rolling exercise began with a violent jerk that brought the person to the ground. Doubled up, the individual would then roll like a wheel or a ball.[83]

Perhaps, the strangest reaction was barking, another form of an outpouring of emotion. A man would get down on all fours near a tree trunk and begin barking, foaming, yelping, or "treeing the devil."[84] Specific breeds were identified from mastiffs to spaniels. Since several men could be barking simultaneously, the noise was electrifying.

There were spectators at camp meetings, some mischievous, and others curious. There could be bootblacks, men selling remedies for a variety of ailments and hawkers of wares that people living in virtual isolation needed. One curious observer visited Cane Ridge in order to gape. James B. Finley, a young man of twenty, found the noise of Cane Ridge deafening:

"The noise was like the roar of Niagara. The vast sea of human beings seemed to be agitated as if by a storm. I counted seven ministers, all preaching at one time, some on stumps, others in wagons, and one was standing on a tree which had in falling lodged against another. Some of the people were singing, others praying, some crying for mercy in the most piteous accents, while others were shouting most vociferously. While witnessing these scenes, a peculiarly-strange sensation, such as I had never felt before, came over me. My heart beat tumultuously, my knees trembled, my lip quivered, and I felt

---

[82] Marianne Sawicki, *The Gospel in History: Portrait of a Teaching Church: The Origins of Christian Education.* New York: Paulist Press (1988), p. 65.
[83] Johnson, *Frontier Camp*, p. 60.
[84] Ibid, pp. 61–62.

as though I must fall to the ground."⁸⁵ Finley fled to the woods to contemplate what had happened. He returned to the camp and witnessed some five hundred people fall and begin to shout and shriek. The scene was too much for him, and again, he fled to the woods, wishing he had stayed at home.⁸⁶ Finley experienced a religious conversion and later became an itinerant preacher. He had an enormous circuit, stretching through the Ohio regions. He spoke at twenty-five places, taking four weeks to make the circuit. Still later, he had to preach thirty-two times on another circuit to more than one thousand members and, in addition, meet with them.

Class meetings and camp meetings were only as effective as the preacher or exhorter. Maintaining control was not always easy. When James Finley dealt with disturbers in his meetings, he would "shake them until their teeth rattled, and pitch them out a window or door."⁸⁷

Since the circuits were so widespread and varied in the quality and temperament of the itinerants, some higher organization was needed. A system of conferences evolved and was critical to maintaining order and discipline. Attendees included class leaders, stewards, licensed exhorters, local and itinerant preachers, and the presiding elder. Issues resolved could be anything from Sabbath breaking to adultery. For serious offences, the sentence was expulsion from the local society.⁸⁸

The conference served as a screening process for clergy and laity. Licenses were renewed for preachers and exhorters. New candidates were examined, and local leaders undertook annual reviews. The white tickets were carefully distributed. If a person's white ticket was revoked, he had to wait until the next quarterly meeting to have it renewed.

The quarterly meeting or conference held three functions: judicial, legislative and executive. While it could not alter doctrinal matters, it could issue general proclamations. One of the more curious

---

⁸⁵ Johnson, *Frontier Camp*, pp. 64–65. Finley, pp. 166–167.
⁸⁶ Ferguson, *Methodists*, p. 136.
⁸⁷ Ferguson, *Methodists*, p. 86.
⁸⁸ Ibid, pp. 89–90.

ones addressed a custom concerning the celebration of Independence Day: "that the attending of barbecues and Drinking of toasts on the Fourth of July is contrary to the Spirit of Christianity and cannot be done to the glory of god."[89]

Originally, the assembly was primarily a business meeting; however, it developed into a combination of business and worship. The one-day gathering was extended to two, and the day was changed to both Saturday and Sunday. This move allowed for people coming from distances to attend. Crowds grew larger and larger, especially if a revival was involved. So while the business meeting was important, it was the opportunity for worship and evangelism that was even more so.[90]

While members of the public did not attend the business portion of the quarterly meeting, they were eager participants in the worship services. The services might include funerals and marriages, in addition to preaching. Itinerant Ezekiel Cooper who had conducted a funeral immediately followed by a wedding remarked that "some are dying others are marrying but soon we all shall be laid in the grave."[91]

Members of the public could view these ceremonies but were drawn by the worship opportunities. Prayer services were well attended, and the impact was enormous. Lester Ruth offers a plausible argument for the extemporary nature of early Methodist prayers. Wesley never meant for the prayer services to substitute for the Anglican *Book of Common Prayer* but to complement it. Eighteenth-century Virginians were largely members of the gentry. Other Methodists may have been less literate and preferred the extemporary method of praying.[92] The person at prayer could use the wide range of their emotions to fully express themselves. And praying was not limited to men alone. Women and even children were recognized as being particularly gifted.[93]

---

[89] Wigger, *Taking Heaven*, p. 91.
[90] Lester Ruth, *A Little Heaven Below: Worship at Early Methodist Quarterly Meetings*. Nashville: Abingdon Press (2000), p. 25.
[91] Ruth, *Little Heaven*, p. 84.
[92] Ruth, *Little Heaven*, pp. 87–91.
[93] Ibid., p. 86.

Unfortunately, few examples of these prayers survive. As in oral history, much of the unwritten word is lost. We only know from observers' accounts how moving these prayers were.

George Coles, a recent immigrant from England, kept a journal recording his astonishment at the tone of the worship services: "the noise on Saturday evening and at Love Feast on Sunday morning was almost too much for me. I hope it was not offensive to Deity but it really seemed indecorous & unnatural." He goes on to say, "[There were] married women without cap or bonnet in the house who think it is no breach of decency to spit on the floor in company. Preachers and others also who after receiving the Holy Eucharist… regaled themselves by spitting pretty freely within the altar."[94]

Early Methodists often expressed themselves emotionally and freely. As they prayed aloud, shouts of amen rang out from fellow believers. For many, this connection meant participating in a fellowship beyond their local society. They were aware that their local place in the circuit meant that they belonged to a greater whole. But it was the quarterly meeting that made this connection meaningful. This sense of identity would change in the nineteenth century as fixed churches and chapels supplanted the earlier itineracy. People became devoted to the local place of worship, and fellowship could be found within these walls and less in the circuit. Although the circuit remained, it was changed as circuits began to be replaced by stations. These units were localized and brought a "parish consciousness" with them.[95] It was not long before buildings became the future of the Methodist Church.

The church is an organic structure, as well it should be. What worked in the eighteenth century changed, as people found permanent homes and wanted a fixed setting for their religious life. Their purpose remained the same: to grow closer to God and receive His assurance and sanctification.

---

[94] Ibid., pp.21–22.
[95] Lester Ruth, *Little Heaven*, p. 185.

Chapter 5

There is neither Jew nor Greek, neither bond nor free, there is neither male nor female: for all are one in Christ Jesus.
—Galatians 3:24

In Christ there is no east or west, in Christ no south or north, but one great fellowship of love, throughout the whole wide earth.[96]

Francis Asbury arrived from England in 1771 just as fears of an upcoming war sent many British citizens back to their homeland. Born to a Birmingham family of modest means, Asbury had only a primary school education and an apprenticeship as a blacksmith forging nails. With no formal training in preaching, Asbury preached his first sermon at age sixteen, having had a religious awakening at fourteen. At twenty-one, he became a full-time Methodist preacher. When Wesley called for volunteers to go to America, Asbury answered his call. Almost immediately, Asbury began his work as an itinerant and succeeded as a missionary. In his lifetime, he preached over 16,000 sermons and traveled 300,000 miles. He frequently traveled with a companion and became so well known that mail was addressed to him simply as "Bishop Asbury, United States of America."

It was in his role as bishop that Francis Asbury excelled as an administrator. Wesley had been denied the power to ordain some ministers for the New World. He consecrated Thomas Coke as the first superintendent, a title Wesley much preferred to bishop.

---

[96] Text: John Oxenham; Music: *Melody African-American Spiritual*; adapt. Henry Thacker Burleigh.

Coke was already a priest in the Anglican Church, so he traveled to America with the intention of ordaining ministers to serve in the new lands. Many British Methodist preachers objected to this irregular appointment, but Wesley persisted, meeting head-on with his brother Charles' disapproval.

> How easy now are Bishops made
> At man or woman's whim!
> Wesley his hands on Coke hath laid,
> But who laid hands on him?[97]

When Coke arrived in America, his intention was to consecrate Francis Asbury as a superintendent. However, Asbury was reluctant as he had not been ordained and arrived in America only as a missionary. His itinerancy was marked with humor and spontaneity, making him a popular figure with his fellow itinerants. His uneasiness over ordination involved their approval. Coke sent Freeborn Garrettson on a twelve-hundred-mile journey to invite preachers to Baltimore for a Christmas conference in 1784, beginning Christmas Eve, the first of ten days of serious business. In three successive days, Coke made Asbury a deacon, an elder, and a superintendent. Other ministers were ordained and authorized to administer sacraments. What followed was to change the nascent Methodist Church in America into an entirely different organization. The Methodist Episcopal Church became an organized body no longer an outreach of the British Methodist Church.

John Wesley had armed Coke with a liturgy suitable for the Methodist Church in America. Its title was clear: "The Sunday Service of the Methodists in North America. With other Occasional Services. London: Printed in the year 1784." The liturgy proposed by Wesley was used for a few years until 1787 when the general conference minutes show it as amended. By 1792, there was no mention of it in the minutes. Most probably, this omission was because the newer Methodists possessed no tradition of the English Methodist Church

---

[97] Ferguson, *Methodists*, p. 31.

that had evolved from the Anglican Church. *The Thirty-Nine Articles of Religion of the Anglican Church* formed a basis for *The Twenty-Five Articles of Religion* for the Methodist Episcopal Church.[98]

Wesley was surprised by the decision to separate from the British Methodist Church. In an effort to assuage him, the Christmas Conference declared that, "During the life of the Rev. Mr. Wesley, we acknowledge ourselves his sons in the Gospel, ready in matters belonging to church government to obey his commands. And we do engage, after his death, to do everything that we judge consistent with the cause of religion in America, and the political interests of these states, to preserve and promote our union with the Methodists of Europe."[99]

When three years later Coke and Asbury introduced a revised edition of the *Discipline of the Methodist Episcopal Church*, the title of superintendent was changed to bishop. Wesley wrote to Asbury: "How can you, how dare you suffer yourself to be called a bishop? I shudder, I start at the very thought! For my sake, for God's sake, for Christ's sake, put an end to all this."[100] Also changed was the 1784 General Conference's clause of obedience to John Wesley in matters of church government. The ties to the British Methodist Church and its founder were officially severed.

Francis Asbury remained the dominant force in the Methodist Episcopal Church until his death in 1816. Unlike Coke, he remained in America while many Methodists returned to England. In total, Coke made nine trips to America, spending less than three years in total.[101]

Despite American Independence, Coke remained loyal to England's King George III and is most remembered as the father of Methodist Missions, having been active in the West Indies. His attempt to reach Nova Scotia to establish missions in Canada ended when a gale brought the ship to Antigua. Subsequently, he sent missionaries to the West Indies, Sierra Leone, Ireland, and France. He

---

[98] Stevens, *History*, Vol 2: Part 25, p. 3.
[99] Stevens, *History*, Vol. 2, Part 25, p. 4.
[100] Ferguson, *Methodists*, p. 182.
[101] Ibid, p. 182.

died on a ship bound for Ceylon, leading a group of missionaries to Africa and India.

During his time as bishop, Asbury exercised extraordinary control over appointments of preachers and their circuits. He also introduced a system of their supervision by "assistants." The 1784 conference enumerated their duties. In essence, they were the bishop's helpers, examining the preachers' suitability in their circuits, the societies, holding quarterly meetings and reporting these findings to the bishop.[102]

While criticized for their control, Asbury and Coke brought stability to the early Methodist Episcopal Church. When a fissure occurred, it was an external threat: the issue of slavery. The Christmas Conference in 1784 declared its position. "We view as contrary to the golden Law of God on which hang all the law and the prophets, and the unalienable rights of mankind, as well as every principle of the revolution, to hold in the deepest abasement, in a more abject slavery than is perhaps to be found in any part of the world except America, so many souls that are all capable of the image of God."[103]

Six months later, there was so much opposition from Southern Methodists that the 1784 rules were suspended. Any attempt to reintroduce legislation to abolish slavery was defeated. The rift between the North and South was too great. And it was not confined to the General Conference.

The quarterly meeting conferences in Madison, Kentucky, reveal the deep divisions recorded yearly. Minutes of the quarterly conference have been preserved for forty-five Madison meetings between 1811 to 1826. Hearings were held on thirteen separate cases regarding the purchase or the sale of slaves.[104]

The deep divide between the North and the South increased dramatically until the split in 1844 when Southern Methodists separated from the Methodist Episcopal Church. The Methodist Episcopal Church, South was a response to the disquieting subject

---

[102] Stevens, Vol. 2: Part 26: p. 17.
[103] Wigger, *Taking Heaven*, p. 140.
[104] Ibid, p. 141.

of slavery. To most of the south slavery was an economic issue. Large portions of the south housed large plantations where cotton was king. Cotton does not pick itself. To plantation owners, slave labor was an economic necessity, not a moral question. Surely, there were exceptions, but generally the success of the economy prevailed.

Concurrent with the ethical dilemma of slavery and the Methodist response was the rise of abolitionism. The movement began in the 1830s and ended in the 1870s, following the Emancipation Proclamation (1863) and passage of the Thirteenth Amendment (1865) and the Fifteenth Amendment to the Constitution. In the 1870s, many abolitionists turned their attention to the women's movement.

Matters came to a head in the 1844 General Conference held in New York. The issue of slavery was originally discussed at the 1784 Christmas Conference. Subsequent conferences discussed the issue with no resolution. The 1844 conference faced a decision that would end the union of the two parties. It came about with the problem of a slave-owning bishop, James O. Andrew of Georgia. Technically, he had inherited two slaves. One was a legacy, a young girl left in his care. At nineteen, she was supposed to be freed and be sent to Liberia. She refused and lived in her own house on his property. The second was a legacy from his first wife, a man who would be freed when he was able to provide for himself.[105] Further ownership of slaves by his second wife complicated matters. Bishop Andrew defended himself, saying he has neither bought nor sold a slave. After thirteen arduous days of debate, a resolution was passed. Bishop Andrew would desist from serving as a bishop. The conference turned to the business at hand: drafting a plan for separation.[106]

The plan for separation was formalized in Louisville in 1845. While the Civil War and its prelude played a part in in the growth of the Methodist Episcopal Church, South, it was the North that profited. Long before war broke out, the General Conference of 1848

---

[105] Ferguson, *Methodists*, p. 224.
[106] Phillip Stone, *How the Methodist Church Split in the 1840s*. Blogs.wofford.edu. (2013).

declared null and void the Separation Agreement of 1844. The issue involved was the Methodist Book Concern and its shared property.

From the very beginning of Methodism in the colonies, Wesley sent books from England, recognizing the value of religious literature. After the revolution and the establishment of a separate church, a press organized to provide books. Preachers would sell them in their travels as agents. The monies would be used to further the publications, and the profits would be distributed to enhance the salaries of the itinerants, retired preachers, their wives and children and widows and orphans. The sum amounted to $750,000 by the time of the court hearings.[107] The Methodist Episcopal Church, South wanted an equitable share.

Three suits for financial recovery were brought, one going all the way to the US Supreme Court. A unanimous ruling in favor of the Methodist Episcopal Church, South, gave them not only funds but also the recognition of the body as a legal entity.[108]

The Methodist Episcopal Church in the North became inexplicably linked with politics. While Francis Asbury and Thomas Coke met with George Washington to plead the case against slavery, it was a meeting with Abraham Lincoln that was more fruitful. The General Conference of 1864 sent a delegation to President Lincoln to pledge the support of the Methodists. Diplomatically, he recognized the support of all churches but added the Methodist Episcopal Church was "by virtue of its greater numbers the most important of all. It is no fault in the others that the Methodist Church sends more soldiers to the field, more nurses to the hospitals, and more prayers to heaven than any."[109]

Northern preachers were sent to the south to exert their influence. Their position was one as a superior who would guide "the

---

[107] *The Methodist Church Property Case: report of the suit of Henry B. Bascom, and others, vs. George Lane, and others*. Richmond: John Early for the Methodist Episcopal Church, South (1851), pp. 1–3. With inflation in 1861, $750,000 grew to 22 million dollars in 2021.

[108] Ferguson, *Methodists*, p. 233.

[109] Ibid., pp. 238–39.

illiterate but warm-hearted brethren."[110] The *Methodist Advocate* went further, urging the northern members not to leave the "poor down-trodden people of the South" in the hands of "the pro-slavery, man-stealing, Negro-whipping, whiskey-drinking, Ku Klux churches to which so many of them belong."[111] This appraisal of Southerners was not new. George Whitefield, evangelist and one of the founders of Methodism, heavily criticized the dancing, cursing, and drinking during his visit to Bath, North Carolina.[112] His appraisal of the rector of St. Thomas Episcopal Church, the Rev. Johannes Garzia, was condescending. The congregation was unfamiliar with his rather vitriolic speech, and instead of hundreds or thousands of listeners, he attracted a hundred.

The organization of Negro[113] Methodist churches began long before the Civil War. The African Episcopal had its roots in the late 1700s but became a separate denomination in the 1810s. The African Methodist Episcopal Zion Church had its roots in the late 1700s and declared its independence from the Methodist Episcopal Church in 1822. Many Africans remained faithful members of the Methodist Episcopal Church. From the early days, freed slaves could be licensed to preach and often became class leaders. The tenets of Methodism appealed to them. The use of the vernacular, singing, and a denomination referred to as "boiling hot" were undeniable attractions.[114]

---

[110] Ferguson, *Methodists*, quoting Ralph E. Morrow, *Northern Methodist and Reconstruction* (East Lansing, Mich., 1956), p. 49.

[111] Ferguson, *Methodists*, p. 248, quoting Hunter Dickenson Farish, *The Circuit Rider Dismounts* (Richmond: 1938), p. 110.

[112] Tim Allen, *A Fiery Preacher in the Old North State: A Tale from North Carolina's Oldest Church*. www.carolinacountry, September 2016. The archives of St. Thomas Episcopal Church illustrate Whitefield's rather condescending attitude toward the Rev. Johannes Garzia, the rector there. And it must have been shocking to Whitefield when the congregation numbered a hundred as he was used to speaking to hundreds or even thousands. *A History of St. Thomas Episcopal Church*. Volume Two, pp.54–55. This work was found in the library of St. Thomas Episcopal Church, Bath, NC.

[113] The term Negro is from the Spanish word for black. In 1793, slaves succeeded in a bloody rebellion on the island of Hispaniola in the West Indies.

[114] Wigger, *Taking Heaven*, p. 129.

That Methodism succeeded is unquestioned. Membership grew at such a rate that Methodists in 1890 accounted for 22 percent of the numbers in all American churches while the South held 34 percent.[115] But while numbers are quantifiable, it was the passion and zeal of those who brought the Methodist message to all that grew the church in this way. Much of Methodism's success must be credited to those who preached a gospel that stirred all people, regardless of race.

---

[115] Ferguson, *Methodists*, p. 260.

Chapter 6

So shall they fear the name of the Lord from the west, and his glory from the rising of the sun.
—Isaiah 59:19

Their Sound is gone out into all lands.[116]

Western expansion of Methodism was critical to its success. Francis Asbury envisioned the march west as an integral part. His view of the church's mission was to pursue the settling of agrarian areas, seeing farming and "frontiersmanship" as ideal callings for Methodists. He was suspicious of city living and its effects. "We have had few city preachers, but what have been spoiled for a poor man's preacher."[117]

The story may be apocryphal, perhaps embellished, but certainly indicative of the Methodists' desire to teach those who did not yet know God. In 1831, four Indians arrived in St. Louis from the area then known as Oregon Territory. Under a treaty of 1818 and renewed in perpetuity in 1827, Oregon was a free country which neither America nor Great Britain owned. Settlers were attracted by free land and a fresh start.

What the Indian chiefs sought was to learn about the White man's religion and to acquire Bibles to take back to their own people.[118] This desire prompted Methodists to forge ahead with their

---

[116] George Frideric Handel, *Messiah*: 2–17.
[117] Access: Dee E. Andrews, *How American Was Early American Methodism?* Princeton, N.J., Princeton University Press (2002), p. 9.
[118] Ferguson, *Methodists*, pp. 151–152.

quests for new territories in which to settle, convert, and spread the Gospel.

Methodism and frontier expansion were not synonymous, but they were simultaneous. Many were simply people seeking a better life. The American revolution of 1776–1783 had destroyed entire towns, and the postwar inflation was rampant. Twentieth-century novelist, Harriette Simpson Arnow gives a vivid description of a people on the move. They "gathered in little groups, squatting, whittling, chewing tobacco, talking, their voices carrying echoes of their lives in other countries. They had smells of leather and horse sweat, baking cornbread, wood smoke, black homemade powder with the sting of burning Sulphur."[119]

The West was a loose description of at first the lands past the Ohio River and later beyond the Rocky Mountains. There was no line of demarcation. The Ohio River became the point of departure for many, despite the government's efforts to keep settlers from crossing.[120] There were two main roads leading to Pittsburgh. Initially built as a military effort, Braddock's Road was 110 miles long and twelve feet wide, attracting settlers from Virginia and Maryland. Forbes Road ran along the western boundary of western Pennsylvania and was 197 miles long and 25 feet across. It was wide enough for one wagon to pass another.

The volume of wagons transporting settlers and their supplies was tremendous. In a village near Pittsburgh where the two main roads met, 236 wagons and 600 merino sheep passed in one day.[121] It was a constant flow of settlers crossing the Alleghenies, seeking better farmland and open spaces.

Some periods saw more rapid migration than others. German immigrants were plentiful due to inheritance laws in some areas of their homeland, affecting large families. The lands would often be divided up into such small plots as to become nonproductive. Likewise, England's system of primogeniture, passing land owner-

---

[119] Harriette Simpson Arnow, *Seedtime in the Cumberland.* New York: Macmillan (1960), p. 223, as quoted in Ferguson, p. 48.
[120] Ferguson, *Methodists*, p. 47.
[121] Ibid, p. 46.

ship to the eldest son, also brought land-hungry immigrants. In addition, political events caused an increase in people looking for a new start. Revolutions in European countries such as Italy and France and events such as the Irish Potato Famine in the 1840s made futures in the New World a necessity for many.

But the determination of Yankees and Southerners contributed to the move westward. A combination of farming errors drove many to settle in new territories. Failure to understand crop rotations and soil renewal caused many to abandon land and migrate. When the wagons reached Illinois, farmers envisioned a new type of farming. Used to toiling in land that was forested with fewer open areas for cultivation, here they found large expanses of prairie and smaller outcroppings of trees making this land more suitable for livestock.

Ownership of land meant that the farmer was free to decide his choice of crops. Initially, it was trial and error as Southerners tried to introduce cotton unsuccessfully at first. But by 1820, corn became the state's staple crop. And by 1840, 22,634,211 bushels of corn were produced, and Illinois stood seventh in production in the union. By 1870, Illinois moved to first place with 129,921,395 bushels.[122]

The size of the early farms was small by later standards, at just 160 acres. Financially, it was risky to begin anew. The first year was often spent in breaking up sod and planting corn and, in September, wheat between the corn rows. The wheat would be plowed between the corn rows and left until spring when the cornstalks would be cut down.

During the second year, more of the prairie might be broken up and planted with wheat, barley, and oats. By the third year, the soil would become even richer with the decomposing grasses and ready for any crops chosen.[123]

While some optimistic observers thought the first two year's work could pay for the new farm and necessary improvements, one farmer-physician in Christian County believed capital was necessary.

---

[122] Richard Bardolph, *Illinois Agriculture in Transition 1820–1870*. University of Illinois Press on Behalf of the Illinois State Historical Society (1908–1984), Vol. 41, No. 4 (Dec., 1984), pp.418–419.

[123] Bardolph, *Illinois Agriculture*, pp. 416–417.

Writing in 1857 for an eastern agricultural journal, he estimated that to establish a new farm of 160 acres the farmer would need $2,500.[124]

In addition to growing corn and grain crops, livestock became important, initially for home use and later for the market. But getting to a market was an obstacle. St. Louis and New Orleans were the two choices. Prior to Chicago becoming a market, farmers used flatboats to ship livestock to New Orleans. Because of river currents, the farmer was often forced to walk the return journey.

The introduction of the railroad changed everything. Prior to 1850, there were several abortive attempts to establish railroads. In 1820, there were twenty-three miles of railroad in the United States. By 1860, there were thirty thousand miles. Early attempts to establish railroads failed due to financial difficulties, despite some government help and private subscriptions. The loss of one locomotive occurred en route to its destination while a second one arrived in Meredosia, Illinois, having been shipped down the Illinois River. The train could be halted by just six inches of snow alone and in the best of circumstances could travel only six miles an hour. The railway passed from one lessee to another until eventually the rails were unsafe to travel.[125]

In 1850, the federal land grant to Illinois, Mississippi, and Alabama ensured the Illinois Central Railroad's existence. A southern Illinois newspaper, *Shawneetown Tri-Weekly Advocate*, wrote with enthusiasm: "The road will be a commercial avenue which will never freeze or dry up. In it here will be no shoals, sand bars, or snags."[126]

In 1851, the Illinois Central received its formal charter, and by 1856, the line was completed. At the time, 705 miles of railroad with 2.5 million acres had been created. The Illinois Central became the longest railroad in the world. The cost was a staggering $26.5 million or $839.7 million in 2021. Much of that cost would come from the sale of bonds in Europe.[127]

---

[124] Ibid.
[125] Martin J. Emill, "*The Illinois Central Railroad and The Development of Illinois*." A Thesis Submitted in Partial Fulfillment of the Requirements for the Degree of Master of Arts in Loyola University, (1933), p. 5.
[126] Ibid, p.41.
[127] Bardoph, *Illinois Agriculture*, p. 41.

The Illinois Central cut a swath of land from Cairo, Illinois, in the south to Galena, Illinois, in the north. A branch line began in Centralia and connected with Chicago. For farmers, it meant accessible markets. Perishable produce could now be marketed and orchards multiplied. Not all were convinced. Some believed that fruit trees could not prosper on the prairies and said, "He who plants pears, plants for his heirs."[128]

The land grant comprised 2.5 million acres. The intent was to sell small grants of land adjacent to the rails. The price of $1.25 an acre rose to $2.50 to farmers and attracted speculators as well. Prices were even less costly through a system of military land warrants for as little as .50 cents an acre. These warrants could be purchased in unlimited quantities through brokerage houses in Boston and New York. In addition, the Gradation Act of 1854 enabled settlers to purchase public domain land for as little as 12.5 cents an acre.

The Illinois Central encouraged investments in large farms from one thousand to twenty-two thousand acres through the sale of its federal land grant property. The division of property along the railway was a checkerboard creation designed by Stephen Douglas, himself an Illinois landholder. The railway held a six-mile territory on each side of the tracks. Plots of land alternated between land retained by the railway and that for sale to the public. The federal land grant of 1851 was divided into even-and odd-numbered plots, the federal government retaining the even.[129] The lots had been divided into 640 acres by the Public Land Survey System. The idea of selling government lands was to encourage the building and use of the railroad. But the potential settlers did not always have sufficient funds to purchase the 640-acre plots, and eventually, the land was distributed through the Homestead Act.

In 1862, after the secession of the southern states, President Abraham Lincoln signed the Homestead Act, freeing up 270 million acres or 10 percent of public domain land. After filing an $18 fee, the farmer received 160 acres with conditions. For five years, he

---

[128] Ibid, p. 421.
[129] Emill, *Illinois Central*, p. 11.

must live on the land, build a house, and make improvements. At the end of the five years, the farmer got the signatures of two neighbors or friends to testify that the improvements had been made. Along with the proof document, the farmer paid a $6 fee, and the land was legally his own.

As the farmers migrated west, they learned new farming techniques. One of the most important discoveries was made by John Deere in 1837. Traditionally, plows had been made of wood. The rich prairie land was difficult to break up, and it clogged the wooden blade with mud. Deere invented a wrought-iron plow with a steel share. The major change to farming came with the railroads. The Illinois Central took advantage of the checkerboard arrangement of land adjoining their tracks and built stations to attract both farmers and later travelers. It wasn't long before towns developed near stations with all the hallmarks of a community. Some were created along ethnic lines, the Germans retaining much of their heritage. German settlements would recreate a town similar to a German village. In Prairie Gem, the German Lutherans and Catholics would find their separate houses of worship. German Protestants originally formed a Missouri Synod congregation, conservative in nature. There would be no drinking or dancing or entering a church of another denomination.[130] In 1890, a more liberal synod took the more liberal members, and they formed a new church. When their building burned, they decided not to rebuild and joined the Methodists. The immigrant Yankees kept their religious affiliations, Methodism among them.

Towns grew as a direct result of the railroads. The Illinois Central planned a station every ten miles. Towns grew up, and schools, banks, local shops, and other amenities created a sense of community, including religion. The churches functioned as centers for both religious and social life in the community. As one can imagine, the Methodists exceeded with their built-in system of class meetings, love feasts, and camp meetings. As an example of the utility of railroads, they enabled attendance at faraway camp meetings.

---

[130] Sonya Salaman, *Prairie Patrimony, Family, Farming and Community in the Midwest.* Chapel Hill: University of North Carolina Press: 1955, p. 88.

Rev. J.S. Inskip, hymnist and later bishop, organized a camp meeting at Vineland, New Jersey, in 1867. The experience of a second coming camp meeting, the sense of receiving a perfect love was shared by people from all over the Northeastern seaboard.[131] The railways brought people together in a way they had never experienced before. The success of this first meeting led to the formation of a National Methodist movement, with Inskip preaching more than forty-nine times.

From the arrival in 1831 of four Indian chiefs in St. Louis by foot to an entire national rail system which by 1867 transported people and goods, just thirty-six years had passed.

The itinerant preacher visiting a lone cabin in the prairies or woods now competed with the growth of fixed churches in towns. The church setting offered a community fellowship for worshipers. Methodist membership grew with the construction of churches. In 1770, there were twenty churches, but by 1860, there were more than nineteen thousand churches with ninety thousand members.[132] The mission remained the same. "Seek ye first the kingdom of God, and his righteousness; and all these things shall be added unto you" (Matthew 6:33).

IC engine should be credited to the Strahorn Museum, Illinois Railway Museum.

---

[131] Ferguson, *Methodists*, p. 278.
[132] *The Methodist Church: Recent Membership Trends*. True Discipleship, 2020.

Chapter 7

And as ye go, preach, saying, The kingdom of heaven is at hand.
—Matthew 10:7

God be in my head, and in my understanding.[133]

If you try to do an online search for either Springbank, Illinois, or the Spring Bank Methodist Episcopal Church, you will come up empty. Actually, you will find two housing developments and an aquatic center in Plainfield, Illinois, named Springbank. Yet there was such a church and a town named Springbank. The Reverend James Thomas Galford, whose sermons are included, became the superintendent in Springbank from 1879–1884.

Reverend Galford was born in Tippecanoe County, near Lafayette, Indiana, on October 19, 1845. He moved with his father, William J. Galford, to Scioto County, Ohio. In 1868 the younger Galford came to Logan County, Illinois, and entered the University at Lincoln, completing one term of studies. He taught school for the winter term and returned to his studies in the spring. In the fall of 1869, he began to teach at the Broadwell School, remaining for two years. In 1871, he returned to Lincoln University, graduating in 1873 with a bachelor of science degree. He returned to Broadwell while also pursuing his ministerial studies.

While a student at the university, James Galford was appointed for one year to the Mt. Pulaski Circuit as a junior minister. In 1874, he joined the conference of the Methodist Episcopal Church and

---

[133] Words: from the Book of Hours (1514). Music: H. Wafford Davies (1910).

was made a deacon. He was appointed to the Schuyler Circuit in 1874 and two years later to the Astoria charge in Fulton County.[134] He was ordained as an elder in 1882. In 1878, he "located." While the term often meant disciplinary removal or inadequacy, his location was marked "on request." The usual reason for a person's leaving the circuit was the desire to settle in one location, get married, and possibly to pursue another occupation. In James Galford's case he followed his interest in farming and ranching.

Also, in 1874, Reverend Galford married Annie Belle Evans, the youngest daughter of David G. Evans. Evans was a prominent member of the Springbank community and was instrumental in the building of the Methodist Episcopal Church there. The cost was $2,200 which today with inflation would amount to over $51,000. Before the church was erected, services were held in private. David Evans would become an important figure in Rev. James Galford's life.

David G. Evans owned one thousand acres of land in Corwin County and had located there in 1851. He built a spacious brick house which was known as "Anchorage Hill." He entertained frequently and counted among his personal friends Abraham Lincoln and Gov. Richard Ogelsby. His home received supply ministers in transit from Springfield or Elkart enroute to their posts. After James Galford married his daughter, Evans deeded to his son-in-law land on which to build a house for his bride.

James Thomas Galford and Annie Belle had five children, the youngest, Thomas, being just three days old when his mother died in 1884. The baby followed his mother shortly and left Reverend Galford a widower with four small children.

Reverend Galford remarried in 1888 to Anne Lydia Wood and had four more children. We are fortunate to have the diary of Anna Evans Galford, a daughter of his first marriage, born in 1875.[135] Written in 1890, it gives us a glimpse into the everyday life of Reverend Galford and his family. She tells of an engaging father, and

---

[134] *History of Logan County, Illinois: Together with Sketches of its Cities, Villages, and Towns, Educational, Religious, Civil, Military, and Political History.* Chicago: Interstate Publishing Company (1886).

[135] Original privately owned by the author.

of life as it evolved on the family farm. The diary begins in January with a weather record as well as some personal notes: "I have done things today which I know I should not."

In February a barn burned, killing three horses. Waiting until spring to rebuild, James Galford hauled lumber from Lincoln. Anna records the men who came to help raise the barn and her amusement that "it seems like cooking for threshers." At various times as a young teen she cooked for twelve to thirteen hay-harvesters, wheat-thrashers, and men hauling corn. She worked hard on the family farm, churning butter, taking care of the chickens, and butchering. Her father made frequent trips to Lincoln and occasionally to Chicago. Much of his travel centered around buying livestock and supplies. Daughter Anna faithfully records attending each Sunday's church service and returning in the evening. At the age of fifteen, she often played the organ at church. Later she graduated from the Illinois Wesleyan School of Music and taught music at Lincoln College.[136] She tells of her father continuing to preach, both at Sunday services and on special occasions. The church was the center of family life and included close relations with relatives who often attended also.

Reverend Galford's life illustrates the changing nature of both the early itinerant preachers and the maturing of the Methodist Episcopal Church as an organization. While the early itinerants were frequently uneducated and of the same social class, they related well to the settlers and migrants. But in Galford we have a minister who is a college graduate, well-educated and well-spoken. His congregation included prominent members of Corwin County who would understand his references to thinkers and scientists such as those he mentions in his sermons. Reverend Galford's congregation reflected the changes in membership that had occurred in Methodist churches. His congregation was varied, including a judge, local businessmen, and both large-and small-scale farmers and their families. As he was a farmer himself as well as a preacher, Reverend Galford shared their

---

[136] Lincoln College was originally known as Lincoln University. In 1901, its name was changed to Lincoln College. In 1929, it became a two-year college, no longer offering a four-year degree. In 2015, Lincoln College returned to a four-year bachelor degree program while retaining the associate program.

concerns. He epitomized the changing nature of the church in the late nineteenth century.

Reverend Galford's sermons often opened with the phrase, "I want to call your attention to…" He suggests approaches and meanings and essentially draws the listener into a partnership, effectively extending an invitation to explore together the topic of the sermon. He is not didactic or dogmatic, nor is he dramatic or overly zealous. His concern is solely the salvation of mankind. He sums up his belief in his ministry when he says, "What we need is not more dogmatic teaching—not a more thorough systematic statement of divine truth—but more of the marrow of the Gospel in the everyday life."[137]

One subject that was extremely important to Reverend Galford was the Sunday or Sabbath School. It is a theme in several of his sermons. Since he had been a schoolteacher, he had decided views on the separation of secular knowledge and religious education. He was a member of the Logan County Teachers' Institute where he spoke on subjects such as mathematics and also "Moral Government in Schools."[138] The purpose of the Sunday school had long been a topic of discussion among Methodists. Only recently was the pastor officially recognized as the head of the Sunday School,[139] and Reverend Galford took this responsibility seriously, as can be seen in Sermon One.

A few author's notes are in order here. In reviewing his sermons, I have chosen not to repeat the underscoring that Reverend Galford used in his written notes in the drafts of some of his sermons. It occurs frequently and is distracting. I would assume that these were markers for him, to perhaps signify inflection or emphasis in making a point when delivering these sermons. I have used italics for a cleaner reading line. Capitalization varies tremendously within the manuscript. At times, "Holy Christianity" will appear and, at others,

---

[137] Sermon One.
[138] *Lincoln Herald*, January 26, 1871.
[139] Fourth National Sunday School Convention as reported in Jack L. Seymour, *From Sunday School to Church School: Continuities in Protestant Education in the United States, 1860–1929*. Washington, DC: University Press of America (1982).

"holy Christianity." I have attempted to remain faithful to the text rather than aim for consistency in modern usage. Similarly, many words that we use hyphenated or even joined together today are written here just as he used them so many years ago. Much has changed in the last century and a half.

There are many places where Reverend Galford leaves an indication that he intends to add an explanation or example. Or perhaps he just paused to let the listener consider and absorb the message. I have chosen to mark these places with [e.i.h.] signifying "elaboration indicated here." We will never know the meaning of these passages and are the poorer for it.

Indentation and punctuation are also considerations in which I have followed the manuscript faithfully. I began to believe that the notation II, etc., were stopping points for him to shift gears and begin a new direction while delivering his sermons. Again, we shall never know the meaning, and no editor can assume otherwise.

Quotations from the Holy Bible conform to the King James Version (1611).

Rev. J.T. Galford lived in unusual times. He saw the Civil War, the end of slavery, the coming of the railways, and what they meant to agriculture and industry. His was a church formed in the crucible of a truly new world. I was privileged to find his sermon book and be able to explore the development of Methodist thinking during this time. Whatever your philosophical or religious beliefs, I hope that you derive a measure of satisfaction, and insight, from this work.

Anchorage Hill, Farm Home of D. G. Evans, Private Collection,

Rev. J.T. Galford, Private Collection.

Sermon 1

For we are labourers together with God.
—1 Corinthians 3:9

This has been a most wonderful and precious statement! When the mind is directed to the idea of *God*, it begins to think of a Being at an immeasurably great distance, clad in the power of its own originality. What a wonderful thought that God recognizes the human agency as worthy of his consideration in the salvation of men and that he brings man up to the plane upon which he condescends to stand, and takes him by the hand and says, "We will work together. I know great difficulties will lie before us. Every power and agency of the Evil One will be used to hedge up the way and to destroy the seeds of truth [even]: but remember this. *I am* with you *Always*. The power that opposes you is infinitely less than that which aids you." If there is one thought above another that should cheer a Christian it is this. That Jesus Christ becomes to him power and righteousness and salvation, and in this places success beyond the *possibility* of a *doubt*. There is no possible reason for failing. Men must not fail. Failure means death and death means here a conscious knowledge of all the possibilities of a *soul* shut up to just one thought ever illustrated—writhing in its own intense agony with the consciousness of absolute banishment from the presence of *God*. What a thought! And yet men are going down to hell with their eyes wide open, accepting the perdition of ungodly men with all the consequences. It was to save the world from this fearful and terrible calamity that *Jesus* came from the Court of Heaven to the sorrows of Gethsemane—to the suffering of Calvary—to the wonderful victory over the grave and to bring life and immortality to light. He commissioned his disciples to go into all the world and *preach* his Gospel with this thought that was to become the talisman of their *power*. "Lo, I am with you always, even unto the end." And this every one today may take as his own watchword which will ensure success.

What we need today is a more thorough conviction in the heart of the need of salvation. Tacitly most men accept the fact that they have a spiritual nature, but there is a very great deal of practical skepticism upon this point.

What we need is not more dogmatic teaching—not a more thorough, systematic statement of divine truth—but more of the marrow of the Gospel in the everyday life. It is only when men appropriate divine truth to their own individuality that they become conscious of its life power; and it is only when they thus place themselves in this relating to Christ and his truth that they see and know the exceeding sinfulness of sin. The world's *need* today is that deep pungent conviction of evil that reveals itself in all its horrid deformity to the *mind*. When this comes to the soul, there is hope that it will be guided up to the Lord Jesus, and by its faith in Christ, Salvation will be realized.

God has commissioned the Church to take the world for himself. And in this human instrumentality, he has *revealed* so much of himself as is necessary for the accomplishment of this object. If there is failure where does the responsibility rest? Is it with *God*? Certainly not. No Christian would presume in his heart to think that God *had* provided a Redemption for men that was defective. Then with the *Church* must rest the *failure*.

This morning, I want to call your attention to one of [the] channels through which and in which these agencies are united—viz, the Sabbath School. And now most of us are wont to look to the time of Robert Raikes for the origin of Sunday *schools* or *schools* for the religious training of *children*.

Let us *read* a part of the sixth and a part of the 11th *Chapters* of *Deuteronomy* and see if from there does not come divine sanction, and that we are to regard it not merely as an *expedient* of human origin for the training of children. For even then while we might *regard* it as an efficient agency, the obligation would be merely optional.

What is the Sunday *school*? This is an important thought for us to settle in the light of divine *truth*.

1) It is not a *Church*. The folly of so regarding it.
2) It is not a place to teach literature. This will incidentally come in; but whoever looks *upon* it in this light would better change for something else or go to the foot of the cross and ask the Holy Spirit to teach him the elementary object of the Sabbath school.
3) It is not a place to teach simply morality. A work in the Sabbath school that comprehends only this idea is very *defective*. There can be no genuine work done in the Sabbath school that does not comprehend moral truth. Morality may be taught without spiritual truth. [e.i.h.]

As to the question "What is the Sunday school?" I would answer it is the training school of the church where spiritual truth is specially to be taught. And as such, it should be under the immediate care of the *church*. God has laid upon the church a heavy responsibility regarding the salvation of the *world*. And here in the tender bud can easily be *shaped* the character that may honor God *and bless the race*.

What attitude must the church assume *toward* that school wherein is trained her young, and wherein those things are taught that makes for man's eternal peace? Clearly, there is but one she must recognize: the relation of *parent* and *child*. And recognizing that much light is thrown *upon* the *work* she must *do*. [e.i.h.]

Settle the question as to *what constitutes the church*.
1) She becomes under God the *proper guardian* of the Sunday school.

   As such the church is responsible for the success or failure that may follow.

   As a *guardian*, she must be ready and willing to *give*:
   a) Her counsel. How much this is *needed*. Some may be *ready* to say *why* not take counsel of God and not of man? *[Answer this.]* [e.i.h.]

b) Her sympathy. There is a magnetism in a *word* that comes unto the weary *toiler's* heart all covered over with love. There is an inspiration about it that quickens him into new life. [Illustrate this thought and dwell upon this *word in general.*] (Obviously a note to Reverend Galford to extemporize.)

c) Her prayers. How important is this when the church before God *agonizes*? The work will be successful and souls will be *saved*.

d) Her money is needed. The burden of the school should not rest on a *few*.

e) Her presence. This thought should be burned deep into every heart. What grand *results* would be *attained* if the whole church as far as it was in her *power* gave her presence to the *Sunday school.*

Then we would not have to discuss the question in the teacher's meeting or official meeting or on the street. How can we develop greater interest in the S.S.? [e.i.h.] With the church alive with holy fire and *zeal* in the *school.* How can it be more efficient would be the question asked. [e.i.h.]

May the God of all grace inspire us with more zeal and more enthusiasm in this *work* of our *Lord.*

Amen.

Results of this work:

a) A full school.
b) A spiritual school.

Sermon 2

Gather up the fragments that remain, that nothing be lost.
—John 6:12

The actual verse reads: "When they were filled, he said unto his disciples, Gather up the fragments that remain, that nothing be lost."

A spirit of *economy* pervading the mind of a man will manifest itself in his relations to others with whom he has to do. He who seeks to put himself in such an attitude to others must utilize every possible means to bring into use all the powers of his being.

Very few if any have such a large endowment of natural tact and ability that they can make the *powers* of their mind conserve to the accomplishment of any great work without great preparation—we might have of even ordinary work.

It is as needful to be economical in husbanding our physical, spiritual, and intellectual powers for the accomplishment of our *life* work, whatever that may be, as to practice it in one single direction—vis., the *financial*.

The history of nations is but the history of the lives of many *men* converging to a given point from which comes the *shape* and character and tone and *life [of]* a government. The history of a single life that has been accredited with any *degree* of true *success* is but a practical illustration of a few generalized truths, all converging to the accomplishment of a given object. Men don't succeed from the great number of principles they may have in their possession but from a *few* that have been thought into the very texture and fiber of their being.

Science had been enriched by many discoveries of Dr. Wollaston.[140] And when asked by a foreign savant to be shown through his laboratory from which had come so many facts for science, he was taken into a little studio and shown an old table, a few watch glasses, an old tea tray, a few test papers, a small balance, and a blow pipe, saying, "That is all the laboratory I have."

It is said of Stothard that he learned the art of combining colors by closely studying the wings of butterflies.[141]

I want to call attention to a few thoughts that are necessary to make our lives a success.

Have a definite object before you.

One half of the failures in the world today grow out of the *fact* that persons have no definite aim and that *work honorable*.

From this comes:

1) Instability.
2) A *general* recklessness in the conduct that *tends* to unsettle all the purposes that may have been *formed* relative to a given object.
3) The road to moral and *spiritual* ruin lies *hard* by "*Aimless Work.*"

Have a definite aim and then let all the influences and circumstances that we may be able to control. Conserve to this one *end*.

Under this thought is the idea of *preparation*.

We should never lose sight of this thought that the religion of Jesus instead of being a hindrance to a man or woman in any work but on the other hand will intensify *and* polish every faculty used for the accomplishment of this *object*.

It should be *thorough*. Much of the world is given to *shams and shoddies*. There is no *business* in which a *man engages if* it is honorable but will be *better* by thorough *preparation*.

---

[140] William Hyde Wollaston was a chemist who discovered how to process platinum ore into malleable.
[141] Thomas Stothard in 1809 discovered a butterfly not previously seen in England.

No *man* has a *right* to follow an *illegitimate occupation because* every unlawful *business* infringes somebody's *right. It is an utter infeasibility* (sic) for a man in business no matter how *low and* mean the *business* or *how* exalted in character it may be to stand *alone*. [e.i.h.]

And in *order* to thoroughness, it *should* be *well rounded*, completed, perfected as far as possible. *And especially* is this true where a man is *called* to the high position of instructing others. [e.i.h.]

The stimulus of other *lives needed* to give encouragement in this *preparation*.

Use every possible diligence to accomplish that *object*.

One very essential thing to be *observed* by any man who *would succeed* is the *law of courtesy*. It costs very little on your *part to be kind, and* it is worth very *much*.

Another is to be *attentive to it*.

Make yourself master of it. The artist saw the struggling *angel* in the *rough* granite and by his hammer and chisel set it *free*.

Sacrifice no principle of *right*, no matter what the circumstances may be. *The reprimand given* by A.T. Stewart[142] to the clerk who misrepresented the *goods*. This implies right principles *formed*. [e.i.h.]

Fix in your mind a strong *determination* to *win. Never give up.* This *dogged perseverance coupled* with the faculty of managing men *and taking* in the situation led Gen. Grant ultimately to *victory.* Cyrus Field and the Atlantic *Cable, Columbus*.[143]

[Thomas] Carlyle says, "Blessed is the man who has found his work: let him ask no other blessedness. Know thy work and do it and work at it like a Hercules. One monster there is in the world—an idle man."[144]

---

[142] A.T. Stewart may have been a local figure.

[143] Galford's emphasis here is on perseverance. Cyrus Field (1819–1892) was a good example of this quality. His initial attempt to lay the first telegraph cable across the Atlantic Ocean (1858) failed when the cable broke afterward. But in 1866, he laid another more efficient and durable cable. Grant fought intensely to achieve his ultimate victory. Columbus' story is well known. Here it seems that Galford was an admirer of scientists and discoveries.

[144] Galford mixes various portions of the chapter on Labour from *Past and Present*. He combines three separate quotations. "Blessed is he who has found his work; let him ask no other blessedness." (p. 190). "The latest Gospel in this world is,

Said Nathan Rothschild to a young man, "Stick to one business young man...stick to your brewery, and you may be the greatest brewer of *London*. Be a brewer, and a banker, and a merchant, and a manufacturer, and you will soon be in the Gazette."[145]

Intense application: Farady (sic), Thomas Edwards.[146] Studying the lives of other men we will find it was largely due to *application. And* in *order* to this, he *must* have *patience*.

"The *angel* of Martyrdom and the *angel* of *victory* are twin *brothers'* is a beautiful *maxim*."[147]

Alexander Hamilton once said to a friend, "Men give me credit for genius: but I can assure you that what they are pleased to call the fruits of genius is the fruit of labor and thought day and night."[148]

John Wesley's life is a commentary upon this thought of *application. Never be unemployed.* He was constantly gathering the *fragments* that nothing might be *lost*.

Know thy work and do it." "Know thyself." p. 190. "One monster there is in the world: the idle man." Thomas Carlyle (1795–1881) was a Scottish historian, mathematician essayist who is probably best remembered for referring to economics as the "dismal science."

[145] What Nathan Rothschild means here, more than likely, is to give a warning against trying too many occupations at once, risking success in one area.

[146] Michael Faraday (1791–1867) was an English physicist and chemist who discovered electromagnetic induction. Thomas Edwards (1599–1647) was a Puritan clergyman.

[147] Iconography in art and architecture often portrays Saint Stephen as the angel of martyrdom and Saint George as the angel of victory.

[148] The actual quotation reads: "Men give me credit for some genius. All the genius I have lies in this; when I have a subject at hand, I study it profoundly. Day and night it is before me. My mind becomes pervaded with it. Then the effort I have made is what people are pleased to call genius." Alexander Hamilton, first sectary of the US Treasury.

Sermon 3

Be it known therefore unto you, that the salvation of God is sent unto the Gentiles, and that they will hear it.

—Acts 28:28

The religion of *Jesus* is of heavenly origin. It was transplanted from its heavenly home to this earth of ours for a special purpose. The keynote of Christ's mission to Earth was *seen* in these *words* and which has been restated with the *same* central thought time *after* time *along* the *ages*. "I came not to call the righteous, but sinners to repentance." [149]

The condition of the Jewish church is fitly represented by these words of Isaiah: "The whole head is sick, and the whole heart faint. From the sole of the foot even unto the head *there is* no soundness in it" (Isaiah 1:5–6).

The only salvation which has the *power* of lifting men out of *sin* and bringing them into a saved relation to *God* is that which *inheres* in our Holy *Christianity*.

God is the Author of this salvation, and as such, he has impressed upon it all the virtues of his own character.

Vice does not necessarily reveal *virtue or* that in order to witness the *perfection* and *beauty* and *power* of a *holy life*. Vice must be put in the background.

The life power of it is another distinguishing feature of it. "In him was *life* and the life was the *light* of men,"[150] could only be said of *Jesus*.

---

[149] Luke 5:32 KJV.
[150] John 1:4.

The purifying *power* of the *Gospel is another* feature of it that separates it *from* all other *religions.*

Its philanthropic or benevolent *element* is another peculiar feature. *This shows* the magnitude of the work [to] the whole *world.*

Another is the character of the reformation it *produces.* It is a radical *change.* It *moulds* the character of *nations* by leaving its own *impress* upon the *mind* of *those* who *govern.*

A thought now upon its character. It is *directly opposed* to *selfishness and* yet brings out the highest possible interest of the individual. This salvation is *sent* to the Gentile *world.* [e.i.h.]

God is the Sender. [e.i.h.]

The objective point in view—the salvation of men. Whatever *results there* are when faithfully *declared* will not *rest* with *man.*

This *designed* to encourage the one who *carries* it. He is *carrying* a system of truths not of his own *creation,* but a *truth* bearing the impress of *God's love and* his *power* for the salvation of *man.*

There is no thought more encouraging to the servant of *God* outside of the knowledge of his *own salvation* than this: that the mission of *love and mercy upon* which he is *sent* is from *God* directly—and the "Lo I am with you"[151] his particularly.

This is of absolute importance to the *missionary* to encourage him to his life *work.*

He *has many and* sure *trials.* It is difficult to enter into the feelings of the *man* who *makes a sacrifice* of *home* and *friends and country* to carry the message of *salvation* to the ignorant and half-savage *heathen.*

It[s] reception by the Gentile *world. "They will hear."*[152] [e.i.h.]

History *confirms* this *statement.* While the *Jew* has stood without the pale of Christianity and contemplated in a cold, philosophic, half *scornful* manner, the *Gentile* has turned to *God* and *found* salvation through Christ.

Our duty to this work. We may not be able to go, but we can help others who *are* willing and *ready.*

---

[151] Matthew 28:20.

[152] The reference here is not clear. There are several passages in the Bible such as Matthew 13:14, Mark 4:12, or Acts 28:26.

Sermon 4

Remember the Sabbath day, to keep it holy.

—Exodus 20:8

An eminent writer upon the observance of the Sabbath has well said that "especially is the Sabbath needful to man as a day of moral and religious being. No elevated state of morals has ever been sustained without it. Mere intellectual culture however severe and refined cannot supply its place."[153] The morals of the Greeks and Romans, even under the most vigorous discipline, became so debased as to subvert their civil institutions. Without the Sabbath, no nation has ever been able to establish and perpetuate free institutions.

God has made provisions for man in establishing the Christian Sabbath. It is not merely the result of arbitrary appointment. Had that been the case, any other day would have answered as well; one day in eight or one day in ten would have *answered*.

After the French Revolution, an effort was made to discard *all* religion and especially all that tended to remind one of our Holy Christianity. They set apart one day in ten. *But* this was found inadequate to the necessities of man's nature, and there was a return to hebdunadal division.[154] And this from practical experience seems grounded in our very nature. We can't live without it.

---

[153] Hubbard Winslow, *Elements of Moral Philosophy: analytical, synthetical, and practical.* New York: D. Appleton and Company (1856), p. 337.
[154] The spelling is *hebdomadal*, meaning consisting of seven days; weekly.

The constitution of animal *life* seems to demand this division. Simply upon the *basis* of our physical necessities, there is an absolute demand for it. [e.i.h.]

Let me direct your minds to this thought.

It is of Divine origin and by Divine appointment.

We read that "on the seventh day God ended his work which he had made, and he rested on the seventh day from all his work which he had made. And God blessed the seventh day, and sanctified it; because that in it he had rested from all his work which God created and made."[155]

1) We notice it reaffirmed by *Moses—and* it was scrupulously taught by *Moses* and the prophets (Exodus 20:8–10).[156]
2) Reaffirmed by our Savior, *and* with that, its true object stated.

There is a necessity upon men to keep this day holy unto the *Lord*.

Physically men *need* it. From this fact, there is encouragement in favor of the present physical arrangement of things that it is from God. But this is of small consideration when we consider the obligation *upon* us as being a *command* from God. It stands in the decalogue. *And* there is not a commandment *here*, but *what* the violation of it involves one in a *crime*.

Take *idolatry*. It is a violation of the *first commandment.*

Take murder, covetousness, adultery—the relation of parent to *child*, etc. [e.i.h.]

1) Its violation *encourages immorality*—not only so but will develop it, because along with a *decline* in the *observance* of the Sabbath, there will be a fostering of almost everything that will appeal to the sensual *nature*.
2) Its violation destroys all *respect* for *Christianity* or the Being who is the Author of Christianity. [e.i.h.]

---

[155] Genesis 2:2–3.
[156] Exodus 20:8–10 concerns the Sabbath. Exodus 20:15–23 are part of the decalogue and ends with idolatry.

A LIGHT REVEALING

Some men seem to entertain the *idea* that a violation of *any divine* is an *insult* to the *follower* of *Christ*. It *may wish* some be intended *as such, but* the *insult* is *offered* directly to God.

Now let us look at some of the *ways* men violate the *Sabbath*.

- By Sabbath excursions.

    No matter *from* what *source*, I lately saw announced through the *paper* that *from* B[loomington] to S[pringfield] a train *would run* carrying pleasure seekers to and from the capital for $1.[157]
- By *keeping open houses* on the *Sabbath*, that *ought* to be *closed*: *saloons, beer gardens*, etc.
- By making it a day of *general festivity*. Roman Catholic *excursion* from the banner.[158]

    Now a *proper regard* for the *Sabbath* will infringe on no *man's right*. Its violation will.

How to secure a proper *regard* for the Sabbath:

By creating a public sentiment against its *violation*. This can *only* be *done* by *Christians* having a proper regard for it *themselves*.

1) By scrupulously attending to the means of *grace* that has been ordained for our *good: not* visiting—*not* doing *any* ordinary work *thereon*, only the doing of those things that *may* involve works of *mercy*. [e.i.h.]
2) By enforcing such *Sunday laws* as will infringe no man's natural *right*. This can *only* be done *when* a sufficient public sentiment *has* been brought into existence that will secure the execution of any right *laws*. [e.i.h.]

A word in *conclusion*: *God* has sanctified this *day* for the *moral* and spiritual benefit of *man*. *Let* us see to that with *us* there is a proper observation of it by having made *the necessary preparation*.

---

[157] There can be no doubt that the Illinois Central changed the habits of churchgoers.
[158] This could possibly refer to festivals where a religious banner is carried.

Sermon 5

Feed my lambs.

—John 21:15

We approach a realm of the kingdom of Christ in considering a few of the thoughts expressed and implied in the above text of paramount importance to the Christian. These words would have had little interest outside of the circle that circumscribed them had they been only human. But coming as they do with the breath of the Almighty upon [them], they form a part of that eternal kingdom of truth which shall never be moved. Standing as we do today it is the distance of eighteen and a half centuries from the circumstances that called them forth. There has been nothing to diminish their authority but very much to intensify their power and beauty and reveal the fact that they come as scintillations from the throne eternal. [e.i.h.] Human life and salvation and happiness are bound up in them.

Jesus recognizes something more in the child than simply flesh and blood. He sees other wants than simply its physical necessities. He said to the wandering disciples *and* thoughtless multitude: "Suffer the little children to come unto me and forbid them not, for such is the *kingdom* of heaven."[159] Not is this all! He took them in his arms and blessed them, and by that mark of tenderness and affection, he has *placed* himself in hearty sympathy with all who work for the salvation of the *child*.

Jesus gave to the church in the *person* of his *disciples* a divine commission to capture the world for *himself* and has hinted through

---

[159] Matthew 19:14 and Luke 18:16.

the text that a diligent search after and oversight over the children will wonderfully facilitate the work.

Character is the result of an unfolding miracle from within the heart either good or bad. It is all important to look at some of [the] things involved in the building up process of our characters. This is what we are before God. We make a distinction frequently—and very nearly as often without any reason—between character and reputation. The realm of the two since they belong to the same man overlap each other in very many particulars. They are both largely bounded with the moral.

From the heart are the issues of life. Out of the heart proceed evil thoughts, murders, blasphemies, adulteries, etc.[160] And as a man thinketh in his heart, so is he. There need be no surprise at this. There must be something behind each act to give it character. Every act of ours has a moral quality or it has not. Every act having a moral quality strengthens the character we are forming.

This is a growth. It strengthens with use. Habits are not formed all at once. They spring not into existence instantaneously but are the result of a gradual unfolding of an impulse started in a given direction. [e.i.h.]

Take for an illustration an expert in *anything*. The facility with *which* he does his *work* is the result of *using* rightly the impulse *started*. [e.i.h.] The influences surrounding us largely affect us and, in very many *cases*, leave their image upon the warp and woof of our lives. This is especially true of *children*. Take as an illustration a family who has been educated and in their conversations in the home *circle* have banished all *slang phrases* or vulgarisms, and not only so *but also* have exerted a positive *influence* against them.

The children will apparently, in an unconscious way, fall in with this and grow up natural grammarians.[161] [e.i.h.]

From *associations* comes this *influence* so great too at times that at the formative period of a child's character such as a bias has been

---

[160] Matthew 15:19 and Mark 7:21–22.
[161] John Locke (1632-1704) in *An Essay Concerning Human Understanding* (1869) asserts the idea of a *tabula rasa* (Latin for an *eased tablet*).

given to it as to affect it materially afterward. [e.i.h.] Take the street education. [e.i.h.]

How powerful this becomes at times.

This *comes* too from an *association* with *books* or rather the authors of *those*. There are very few *original men*. This is true everywhere in every department of industry *or in every* vocation of life. [e.i.h.] The human being is not born with real knowledge but gains it through experience. This being true, we are affected very materially by coming into contact with others, either personally *or through their writings*.

Why the writings of so many are *polluting*.[162] [e.i.h.] We see only a *picture* and not the *thing*. Then they appeal to the worst phase of the child's life, and he leaves to associate all that he conceives to be noble and manly with that which is low and vicious.

A right impulse given to a heart followed by a constantly increasing effort to strengthen that impulse will not fail of accomplishing the end in view. [e.i.h.]

The wise man has said, "But the path of the just *is* as the shining light that shineth more and more unto the perfect day.[163]

"My son attend [to] my words; incline thine ear unto my sayings. Let them not depart from thine eyes; keep them in the midst of thine heart. For they are life unto all those that find them, and health to all their flesh."[164]

Now this first must be from without. [e.i.h.] The teaching *imparted* is such an external *impulse*. "Train up a child in the way it [he] should go, and when it [he] is old, it [he] will not depart from it."[165]

The *teacher* sustains about the same *relation* to the child that the vinedresser does to the vine. The mind is *plastic* and can be *moulded*.[166]

---

[162] It is interesting that Reverend Galford crossed out the word 'fictious' before 'so many'.
[163] Proverbs 4:18.
[164] Proverbs 4: 20-22.
[165] Proverbs 22:6. Reverend Galford substitutes *it* for *he*.
[166] Again, a reference to John Locke.

Take the training of the *Wesleys* as an *example*. *John Wesley* was a *child* who had *been* instructed by his mother and *one thing* she had [taught] *over* and *over*, and no *impression* seemed to *have been* made, when her husband remonstrated with her about spending so *much time* with so dull a boy, etc. [e.i.h.]

The conversion of the *infidel* who *casually* came to [B's] church *and* who prepared a special *sermon* for *him* but who was converted *from* the simple *remark* of an old *colored lady*.[167] [e.i.h.]

This *teaching* must be followed by *example*. Teachers who *teach simply* by precept are much *like* the *index* or a *guide board* when you get on the opposite side of the street and look at *it*.

They print in an opposite direction *from* the *reading*. [e.i.h.]

The surroundings of men have much to do with giving a healthful impulse to their conduct.

Who are the responsible agents for the right training of the youth?

This is an important question. We do not propose in the brief time here to consider [it] in all of its bearings *but* to indicate a few thoughts.

The state should feel a deep interest in the welfare of the child for in that child is the future *active subject*.[168] He falls into the *niche* awaiting him then to exert a healthful or unhealthful *influence* upon those surrounding him. The state has provided means for the education of the child. But even here, the question arises. What shall be the character of the education provided for the child? To say the most for it, it can *only* be of a moral character, with all that *intensifies* morality left out. And here is the basis of the division of *Protestants* and *Catholics* or for that matter of any who stood opposed to the Bible.[169]

The *church* is responsible directly under God for the right training of the child. Her work is essentially spiritual. And this lies at the foundation of every other. [e.i.h.]

---

[167] The reference here is unknown. It could possibly refer to Bloomington.
[168] The role of the state was a popular subject for discussion.
[169] Catholics place a great emphasis on religious education as part of the general curriculum.

The business of the state is to so guide the *moral* faculties of man that he may become a good citizen of the country to which he belongs; to him recognize those relations that make for his temporal well-being. That of the church to so guide the soul of man that he becomes a faithful follower of the *Lord Jesus* and to recognize and practice those things that make for his eternal *peace*.

When we see what the Sunday *school* is designed for, we can see what attitude the *church should* sustain to the *school*.

1) It is a place where spiritual truths are taught. [e.i.h.] Each person enters here with the conscious knowledge that while such teachings might be interdicted in the public school, there is no limitation here. He takes his Bible and class and talks to them about Jesus.

2) It is the training school of the church. One-half of those who come into the church today are from the Sunday school. And where there is good faithful work those who thus enter will become shining lights in the cause of God. [e.i.h.]

   The Sunday school is not separate from the church or independent of it but a *part* of it. What she does is not so much to build up the S.S. as to build up the cause of Christ.

   The church under all circumstances where there is faithful work done will reap the fruit.

   Enlarge this thought to *some extent*. And now this involves the last thought I want to call your attention to.

   The attitude the church should sustain to the *Sabbath school*.

   She ought to have an immediate oversight over the school. The necessity for this grows out [of] the fact that a school will die out unless there is such a relation recognized. [e.i.h.]

3) She ought to provide for the necessities of the school.

   This is a very important feature that is frequently overlooked. There are papers and books, lesson papers, etc.

needed to make a school interesting and help keep up the life of it.

4) She should be given her *counsels* and *prayers* and sympathies and leave off her fault finding. [e.i.h.] This means she should *properly control* that committed to her care.

When these relations are properly recognized and faithfully executed, then [we] may expect and see a mighty harvest of souls for God. Amen.

Sermon 6

And the blood shall be to you for a token upon the houses where ye are: and when I see the blood, I will pass over you, and the plague shall not be upon you to destroy you, when I smite the land of Egypt.
—Exodus 12:13

We have in this C. [chapter] the unfolding of a truth that was to bring the children of Israel into a more intimate relation to God.

Israel had been greatly honored in Egypt. Joseph had so guided the government during his administration as chief secretary of state that the most wholesome laws both for the Egyptians and Israelites had been enacted and executed. But his reign had an end and with it came the end of that government that was so necessary to the healthful development of this people. [e.i.h.]

There is instituted a *kind* of government after the death of the then ruling sovereign that found its end in the *most* absolute and shameful tyranny. Those foreigners instead of becoming citizens have been reduced to the most absolute *slavery*. From all over that land comes the pitiful wail of an outraged and insulted people, grinding under the most galling yoke of oppression.

We can scarcely conceive of a people brought down so severe to the lowest stratum of degradation than these proscribed *Israelites*. Their cup of suffering has filled to its full.

God, who watches with a *jealous* eye over his own hears their cry and determines on their release. He sends them *one* who has not only been educated at the imperial court but who has in the land of *Median* in the great retreat of a shepherd's life learned the invaluable lesson of governing his own life. He is commissioned to go in the name of the "*I Am that I Am*" and procure the release of these people. How wonderfully doth he doeth! How grandly does he do the work God has committed to his keeping! How majestically does he rise above the oppressing difficulties that seem to hedge up his way at every *step*. Notwithstanding the hypocrisy of the astrologers, the studied deception and chicanery of the court, and the ingratitude of his own countrymen, he plods on, hopes on, and prays on faithfully doing his work; and [en]trusting his cause in the hands of the All-Father who is watching and guarding this faithful *servant*. He too, amidst his work, catches with a prophetic eye a glimpse of the Son of God. As amidst the moral gloom gathering like midnight darkness around this people, he builds up a ritualistic service that sends its healing streams—its life and light and joy and peace out through the Passover that was to commemorate their deliverance from *slavery* and *sin* and *shame*.

I want this morning to call your attention to a few thoughts suggested by the twenty-first verse (sic). "And the blood shall be to you for a token upon the houses where ye are: and where I see the *blood* (sic) I will pass over you, and the plague shall not be upon you to destroy you when I smite the land of Egypt."

The *general* thought and the one withal I wish to impress upon your mind is that exemption from spiritual death is *only* obtained through the blood of *Christ*. This *blood* of the *lamb* was only the typical blood, and its vitalizing and cleansing power came from the one it *typified*. There is no remission of sins without the shedding; and that blood only became powerful to save in so far forth as it *was* connected with *Jesus*.

The Passover was only beneficial *and only* saved when the conditions were complied with. [e.i.h.]

We must have faith in the Word that says the threatened punishment will be executed. This implies *action*.

We must make the necessary preparation for the *Supper*. What the preparation implies. *Dwell upon the preparation. Read* carefully here the third to tenth inclusive. [e.i.h.] *Dwell upon the sprinkling of the blood upon the door posts.*

We must *eat* the *Passover*. Here is the crowning act of his faith. But the question and an important one: how shall he eat it? What is the particular meaning to him? [e.i.h.] "And thus shall ye eat it with your loins girded, your shoes on your feet, and your staff in your hand; and ye shall eat it in haste; it is the Lord's Passover" (Exodus 12:11). What would be the objector's position if such be found?

The Christian's Passover is Christ, and the practical and *real* benefit derived from this grows out of a hearty *compliance* with the *conditions*. [e.i.h.]

We have these formulated expressions of our Savior which *answer* the real condition of man. He that believeth on the Son hath everlasting life.

He that believeth not shall not see life, but the *wrath of God abideth on him.* [e.i.h.]

This brings salvation to the believing *heart*. This salvation is of a spiritual nature. He will save his people from their sins.

Another thought is there must be a fulfilling of all the conditions. The same objections might be *urged* that we suppose some urged at that time. *A partial work.* [e.i.h.]

Whenever we begin objecting to this phase of Christian truth or turning away from that divine requirement, we simply reject the atonement for sin made by our Savior and *institute a salvation of our own*. Every such work will be fraught with the gravest *consequences*.

Then there will be the sprinkling *of the blood*.

May we all realize the *blood* sprinkled upon our own *hearts*.

Amen.

Sermon 7

The blind receive their sight, and the lame walk, the lepers are cleansed, and the deaf hear, the dead are raised up, and the poor have the gospel preached to them.
—Matthew 11:5

The burden of the preaching of Christ is in the salvation of men—the bringing of them into a condition of *new life* producing the beneficial result of "reconciliation" to the divine *will*.

There is an energy of power and purity about the doctrines of our Holy Christianity that could not be felt in the human life, even if not that Jesus has left the breath of his own pure and spotless life upon them. No more can we put ourselves into direct contact with the electric battery when it is surcharged to its upmost capacity and not feel the effect of it on our bodies, than we can put ourselves in an immediate relation to Christ and his truth, honestly and heartily, and not feel the uplifting power there is in this gospel of *Christ*. No one ought to bring a charge of weakness against that which claims to be the embodiment of all that is powerful if he has never thoroughly tested it. There are certain principles that underlie our attitude to anything and everything that challenges our attention and, which if we failed to apply these to the questions in hand, would convict us before the world of consummate duplicity. It is not only the height of folly but also of ignorance and not only infrequently of maliciousness to give character and audience to a report founded simply on rumor that involves the character and honor of another.

The question for us is and which will have a wonderful modifying influence upon our relations to the report is, is it true? What are the circumstances or conditions in the matter? The same law of truth holds respecting our relations to the truths of the Gospel.

He who attempts to put himself in relation to a principle to test its validity and who fails of realizing the truthfulness of that principle would be a more competent witness than he who had never made the trial; but he who has made the trial and has a conscious knowledge of its life power in his own individual experience is a much more competent witness than either of the others can possibly be. Such must be the attitude of every true follower of the *Lord*, not only in his relation to gospel truth but also in his posture to the world. We can but see the effects of gospel truth upon the hearts of men, look in whatever direction we may. Its distinguishing features reveal itself at every step of its development in the soul. It's the uprising in the soul of a better and nobler life. There is such an impulse given to the heart of man that he rises to a position morally and spiritually that could not be attained without the text Jesus gives to John's disciples to unfold to him the real mission of the gospel in the world. "The blind receive their sight and the lame walk, the lepers are cleansed, and the deaf hear, the dead are raised up, and the poor have the gospel preached unto (sic) them." How wonderful this work! How far reaching in its purifying power! John evidently must have been satisfied when such an answer comes involving such wonderful results of power and character and life—the objective points of a *life* and mission of which was the forerunner. I want to call your attention to a few thoughts.

The light of the Gospel. [e.i.h.] I am the light of the world, said Jesus, "He that followeth me shall not walk in darkness but shall have the *light of life*."[170]

The only character in the gospel that shines by its own inherent light with ever increasing splendor is Jesus. "I am the light of the world" is not a mere statement involving a truth abstractly considered but one of the highest practical utility affecting your destiny and mine.

Men love darkness, said Jesus, because their deeds are evil. [e.i.h.] They will not come to the light lest their deeds become manifest.

---

[170] John: 8:12.

A LIGHT REVEALING

Without this *light*, the world would become total darkness—mentally, spiritually, intellectually, socially. It is sometimes difficult to understand why the dwarfing of one part of our nature affects the whole man. [e.i.h.]

There are certain loyalties where there is an almost total absence of this *light* in which sin in all its horrid deformity is revealed, bringing to view the most loathsome spectacle of human degradation and suffering. [e.i.h.]

There may be an absence of this light in the individual heart, but the general influence exerted lets some ray fall athwart the sinner's path that lights the darkness that would soon end in eternal gloom.

He is so the Light of the *Gospel* that no one *else* can possibly sustain this relation to the world except this light being transmitted to them. "Ye, the light of the world,"[171] said Jesus to his disciples. But here it is only in the sense that they came in contact with them [him] and received that which he was ready to impart.

He is so the light of the world that he *freely* imparts to others this *light*, and to them it becomes a living fact in the life. *And* not only so but also on his part he imparts it without money and without price. Others most *generally* in possession of that which will exert a salutary influence upon others expect to be remunerated. [e.i.h.]

The life of the Gospel is Christ.

It needs no extended argument to show this as true. [e.i.h.] "*I am* the way and the truth and the *life*" (John 14:16). *In him was life.* With thee is the fountain of life."[172] Not only is it true that he is the life of the world, but also it is true that had not Jesus come, the gospel would never have been preached as the saver of *life* unto *life* to those who *believe*. [e.i.h.]

This life is not *simply* of that *character* that stamps itself upon any biography that may be written, but that character of which when

---

[171] Matthew 5:14–16. The "I" was changed to "we" in this sermon. This became a Christian gospel hymn in the 1960s.
[172] Psalm 36:9.

I reach out by faith and lay hold upon it, I become conscious of its life power in my own heart. [e.i.h.]

The power of the Gospel is Christ. "I am not ashamed of the gospel of Christ," said Paul, "for it is the power of *God* unto salvation to every one that believeth; to the Jew first, and also to the [Gentile]."[173]

John would understand what was meant by "the poor have the gospel preached unto them."[174] [e.i.h.] The glad tidings from heaven was the *gospel* of peace.

1) This power is seen in the *direct* and immediate work upon the soul. [e.i.h.]
2) In the work of binding the affections of men to the throne of God, [e.i.h.] God has recognized this as the only sure way of keeping men out of hell. [e.i.h.]
3) This Christ power intensifies the life of the Christian and causes it to become fruitful in honoring and glorifying the name of God, and in helping with the path of righteousness, the unsaved.
4) This power too is seen in its manifestation in the believer's life, in giving to him the true idea of *salvation* in this, that the *life* of the saved man will be used to make the world better, helping the sorrowing and *distressed*. The wrong idea of salvation is we are inclined to *want* the *grace of God* in our heart, to use it for our own pleasure. Pleasure and happiness will come to us as a result of our work to save others.

Amen.

---

[173] Romans 1:16.
[174] Matthew 11:2–3.

Sermon 8

Can any man forbid water, that these should not be baptized, which have received the Holy Ghost as well as we?
—Acts 10:47

The *design* and mode of baptism [and also obligation].[175]

1) It was designed as the inductive *rite* into the visible Church. [e.i.h.] As circumcision to the Jew was the inductive *rite* into the *Jewish Church*.

   It is contended by many that the objective point of baptism in the mind of the disciples was remission of past sins. [e.i.h.]

   By others that it is the rite inducting us into the visible Church, whereby the subject has signified the fact too of an inward work being done in the *heart*.

2) The *mode*.

   This is left largely optional with the subject. The custom varies with the age. *The baptisms* of ancient *times under* the Mosaic law was by *sprinkling. Under the newest age by immersion* and yet a *critical notice* of the *words* in *use indicate sprinkling.*[176]

---

[175] The words in parentheses have been crossed out.
[176] The argument is ongoing—whether infant baptism or adult is better. Should a being be cognizant of the consequences? The idea of infant baptism is more akin to the earlier rituals of the Catholic Church, fearing the departure of a soul in infancy before being accepted as a member of the body of Christian believers.

3) The *obligation* of *baptism*. *This rests* upon the *authority of Jesus* in the *commission*, the *disciples* in their *preaching*.

A second *thought* I want to call your *attention* to and which is of paramount importance.

The immediate work of the *Holy Ghost upon the believing heart*. The *certainty* of the *gift*.

1) I want to remark [on] this thought. The work of the Holy Ghost is an actual and real work. It is not necessary to discuss the question as to the personality of the Holy Spirit.

    The commission—Jesus's words to his disciples—the Comforter. [e.i.h.]

    It may be mysterious and yet it is *real, the electric current*.

2) His work is direct, immediate and constant. [e.i.h.] He operates directly upon the *heart* and not through any third party. [e.i.h.] The conditions having been complied with, it becomes *immediate*. Not only that but it is a constant work. The apostle speaks of this constant work in the testimony he bears to the believer of his acceptance. [e.i.h.]

    One *result* of the *work* to the *believer* is his *power* with *God. All things* are possible with *God*, and we enter the realm of the *possible* in proportion as we rise up to the full stature of men and women in Christ *Jesus*. [e.i.h.]

3) Another *result* is the *sealing* of the believer in Christ unto the day of *redemption*. We are sealed by the spirit of promise. [e.i.h.]

4) Another is the purifying *effect* upon the *heart* by our faith in the *blood* of *Christ*. [e.i.h.]

    [There is nothing to indicate the completion of the sermon—no summation, no closing prayer or amen.]

It is fairly obvious that Reverend Galford favored baptism at a time when the inductee was cognizant of the benefits and obligations therein.

Sermon 9

*Therefore whosoever heareth these sayings of mine, and doeth them,
I will liken him unto a wise man which built his house upon a rock:
and the rain descended, and the floods came, and the winds blew, and
beat upon that house; and it fell not: for it was founded upon a rock.
And every one that heareth these sayings of mine,
and doeth them not, shall be likened unto a foolish
man, which built his house upon the sand:
And the rain descended, and the floods came, and the winds blew,
and beat upon that house; and it fell: and great was the fall of it.*
—Matthew 7:24–27

These words close our Savior's "Sermon on the Mount." The wondering multitude stand before Jesus filled with astonishment at the words that have fallen from his lips. Their verdict is: "Never man spake as this man." And what was there peculiar about this teaching that led the multitude almost involuntarily to give expression to a thought that has been *confirmed* in every age since?

What is there about the truths underlying our Savior's work—truths that were restated by him or created anew that have attracted the whole civilized world, either to find some measure of praise for them or to utter some word of condemnation?

Jesus stands before the world as *The Character* who has the *power* of placing himself alongside of humanity in a life-imparting attitude. His words and his teachings have received the divine *image* of his person. In living letters, by the blood of the everlasting *covenant* is written the guarantee for your salvation and mine.

Hear him as he unfolds to the multitude these precious truths that came freighted with life and salvation. "Blessed are the pure in heart, for they shall see God. Blessed are they which do hunger and thirst after righteousness, for they shall be *filled*." Upon the ear of him who had been accustomed to listen to lectures or sermons involving only moral questions or the interpretation of some prophecy which to say the least was doubtful, these words of our Savior must have had a wonderfully startling effect.

Jesus calls the attention of the wondering multitude to two characters, these illustrating the character of two great classes who are within the reach of salvation. One who has voluntarily accepted Jesus—the other who has virtually rejected them. [e.i.h.]

They *both did something*. Jesus is particular to specify what each did so that there will be no mistaking the cause of failure or success.

You will mark the language—the work they did—the character of it is based upon the thought *expressed by* "*them*." The *one heard* but acted upon the instruction given. The other *heard and acted* upon some *other* line of thought.

The doing implies a previous instruction.

They *both heard*. [e.i.h.]

Hence there was an equality between them both so far as this was *concerned*.

Jesus recognizes the fact that the limit of human responsibility ends with the *possibility of knowing*. [e.i.h.] "If I had not done among them the works which none other man did, they had not had sin" (John 15:24).

The light of the Gospel shone upon them. [e.i.h.]

The advantages of this truth coming to the *Soul*. [e.i.h.]

They both had convictions. Now it seems to me here was the point of *divergence*. [e.i.h.] The one *acts* up to his convictions. The other fails. [e.i.h.]

This let me say is of the highest utility to all. If one is loose in his *conduct* respecting his convictions of right, it will cast a shadow over his entire life and materially affect those with whom he may come in contact. [e.i.h.]

The *loss is irreparable*. [e.i.h.]

A LIGHT REVEALING

There are some thoughts here I want to call your attention to. They materially are of paramount importance to all who have a desire to make a success out of their *life*. The saddest part of this is the loss to be sustained.

Stand beside that criminal as he is about to be launched into eternity for his *crimes*. Contemplate the possibilities that have been bound up *here*, and then look at the absolute *failure*. The thought as it comes to my *soul* is of a sorrowful nature. Last winter and the man from Rock Island who was engaged in the whiskey *business*. [e.i.h.]

1) Men don't *fall all at once*, i.e. the precipitation into ruin may be immediate, but the causes that have produced these sorrowful results have been forming for months and years possibly. [e.i.h.]

    Wrong doing is cumulative. Sin is sure *and* rapid in its development unless some counteracting agency destroys its *power*. [e.i.h.]

2) It has no refuge in time of storm to shelter those who place themselves under its power.

    It is *deceptive* from the fact that the inevitable result of sin when *completed* is absolute and certain *ruin*. It is *deceptive* because it comes to men with the glamour of intelligence. [e.i.h.]

How many misguided men have made their bed in *hell* with the thought that Christianity was a senseless bundle of *fables*. [e.i.h.]

The last thought: the life of the man grounded upon Christ is proportionally as great as the loss of that one built up out of *Christ*. Both involve results that are *eternal*. [e.i.h.]

The certainty of success of the *life* in *Christ* is implied in the *idea* of the building *upon* the *rock*.

May the *God* of all grace *bless* his truth to the *heart*. [e.i.h.]

Amen.

Sermon 10

We know we have passed from death unto life, because we love the brethren.

—1 John 3:14

John in the fifth chapter of the letter gives us this language: "Whosoever believeth that Jesus is the Christ is born of God: and every one that loveth him that begat loveth him also that is begotten of him. By this we know that we love the children of God, when we love God, and keep his commandments. For this is the love of God, that we keep his commandments: and his commandments are not grievous" (1 John 5:1–3 KJV).

He who would *know* the truth must place himself in such an attitude to God that the truth to him becomes a conscious entity in his soul. It is idle to talk of things being certainties that lie wholly within the realm of the imagination. For anything to become to us positive knowledge must not only be founded on fact, but must have behind it an authority and an intelligence that bring an assurance of the fact. Paul writing to the Thessalonians says, "For our gospel came not unto you in word only, but also in power, and in the Holy Ghost, and in much assurance."[177]

There are certain criteria in physical facts that we must *know* before certain things *come* to us as positive knowledge. There are in the realm of the spiritual certain criteria which each one can apply to his own individual *case*. "If ye love me, keep my commandments," said Jesus. "And I will pray the Father, and he shall give you another

---

[177] 1 Thessalonians 1:5.

A LIGHT REVEALING

Comforter, that he may abide with you for ever. *Even* the Spirit of truth; whom the world cannot receive, because it seeth him not, neither knoweth *him:* but ye know him; for he dwelleth with you, and shall be in you."[178]

Jesus said again, "If a man love me, he will keep my words; and my Father will love him, and we will come unto him, and make our abode with him."[179]

"He that hath the Son hath life."[180] *And w*hosoever are turning to the same thought, we have given another quotation "believeth that Jesus is the Christ is born of God."[181]

There is implied here in all this teaching a knowledge of our acceptance with *God* that amounts to an absolutely certainty. [e.i.h.]

The *character* of the *work* done in the salvation of man. [e.i.h.]

There are various ways of speaking of the work with a reference to the character of it. One thought is: *the work is Real,* i.e. it is an actual fact. [e.i.h.]

It is in *accord* with the teachings of *Jesus*. For instance: Mark last chapter—Paul at Crete—the skeptical. How we are to interpret this? The *influence upon the heart* is in *accord* with the teachings of *Jesus*. [e.i.h.]

It has an actual and *real life power* about it in its cleansing work upon the *Soul* of which the person is not conscious at the time of its operation in this work *but* is positively certain as to results if certain *laws* or conditions are made the basis of action. [e.i.h.] *Hence* it is *not* an imaginary *work*. [e.i.h.]

There is a divine progression in this work. [e.i.h.] *But* then what is the *character* of this *progression*? What is the character of *progression* in general? *Unless* there is an *advance* to *something higher* and better it is useless to talk of this. [e.i.h.]

And now a word or two *upon* the expression. "From death unto life." Why the thought "from death unto life?"

---

[178] John 14:15–17.
[179] John 14:23.
[180] 1 John 5:12.
[181] 1 John 5:1

Sin is *linked* with failure, ruin, and death—everything that *dries* up the *issues* of the *Soul. That* which counteracts it or destroys its effect is the *essence* of *life* and *power* and *success*—everything that brings out the best possible side of the human *element.*

And now can we today say, "We *know* we have *passed* from death unto *life*." [e.i.h.]

Amen.

Sermon 11

Because there was no room for them in the inn.
—Luke 2:7

These words are very suggestive outside of the mere statement that they refer particularly to the birth of Jesus. When applied to Christ—there is much in the world that practically illustrates them. I want to call attention to this thought.

There is nothing that in the smallest conceivable degree affects our interests here but what the principles of our Holy Christianity will place on a more solid basis if they are carried into it. [e.i.h.] Jesus gave to the world his gospel and breathed upon it his own pure spirit that it might bring men and women up to a point that would result in developing true manhood and womanhood. This is seen in the *law* given by *Moses*.

This too is seen in the Sermon on the Mount and the general teaching of *Jesus and* in the writing of the *Apostles*.

He is virtually excluded in every thing where there is not a hearty recognition of his *authority*. [e.i.h.] "Ye cannot serve God and mammon."[182] *There* can be no *division*.

There is no room for him in much of the conduct of the nominal *Christian*. A nominal Christian is little more than another name for formality or *Phariseeism (sic)*.

"*Unless* your righteousness *exceed* the righteousness of the Scribes and *Pharisees* ye cannot enter the kingdom of heaven."[183]

---

[182] Matthew 6:24.
[183] This is a paraphrase of Matthew 5:20.

They who have a *form* of *godliness*. [e.i.h.]

There is no room for him in *much* of the so-*called* social life of *men*.

We are social *beings*. *God* has recognized this *fact*. *But* there is *much* in the *conduct* of *men* herein this that *tends* to *ostracism*. Here as *much* as anywhere is seen the tendency to the formation of *castes*.

There is no room for him in much of the business transactions of men, [e.i.h.] even under the *head* of that which is legitimate.

The *incident* of the *boy* selling *gloves*. *Reproved* by his *employer*. [e.i.h.]¹⁸⁴

Christianity recognizes the *fact* that men *should* conduct *business upon* Christian *principles*. "Do unto *others* as you would have others do unto you."[185]

What *shall* we *say* of all that is questionable? The least able to say.

There is no *room* for *Christ* in much of *the legislation* said to be done *ostensibly* to *elevate men and* protect *them* in their *interests*. [e.i.h.]

Phillip II *conduct* while *King* of *Spain*. [e.i.h.][186]

England's conduct toward Puritans and C.[187] Even here in our land. [e.i.h.] The methods of lifting man into office.

There is no *room* for Christ in the *follies* and *vanities* of the *world*. How broad the door here and how man go in there all. [e.i.h.]

Where the principles of the *gospel* are *excluded from* any of the relations that affect us *here*, the responsibility is wholly on the human side. *Men will not* seems (sic) to be the common *verdict*. [e.i.h.]

"*And ye will not come to me, that ye might have life*" (John 5: 40).

---

[184] This must be a local reference.

[185] Luke 6:31. Matthew 7:12. The Golden Rule is not written as such in the Bible.

[186] Reverend Galford could have been referring to any number of Phillip's exploits. As the Catholic King of Spain, Phillip II is remembered for his roles in the Counter-Reformation, the Inquisition, his marriage to Mary Tudor or even the imposition of a ten percent sales tax to shore up his military budget.

[187] One may assume the C. in this note refers to Calvinism. Pilgrims' Hill on the River Dart in Devon was the site where they would be in quarantine to avoid "contaminating" local residents who lived nearby. The weather being so unpredictable they were forced to remain until passage on the Mayflower was calmer.

Sermon 12

This is a faithful saying, and worthy of all acceptation, that Christ Jesus came unto the world to save sinners; of whom I am chief.
                                                                1 Timothy 1:15

The objective point of Christ's *coming* was to *save* man.

Salvation *implies [that it]* can only *take* place with those who are without it—are lost. [e.i.h.]

This salvation was brought to us. Christ came that men might have *life*. *We ought* to be *grateful*. [e.i.h.]

This salvation is peculiarly of a human character. [e.i.h.] It was not designed for angels—but men. Christ took upon *himself* the form of a *man*—a *servant*.

This salvation is *universal*. To save *sinners*—all *sinners* who will come *unto him*. God's arm is not shorn of its *strength*. [e.i.h.]

The *character* of this *salvation thus brought* to *men*.

It is preeminently spiritual. By *that*, I mean it specifically comes to the spiritual nature of man. [e.i.h.] *Now there* is *much* in the world attributed to *God* that belittles *him*.

Its power to save reaches to the farthest limit of man's necessity. He saves to the uttermost all that come unto *God* by *him*. [e.i.h.] Though your sins be as scarlet, they shall be as white as *wool*.

It *overcomes and* heals the *most malignant character*. [e.i.h.] Paul speaks himself as being the chief of *sinners*.

It assimilates itself to the individual *and* leaves the *character* of its author imprinted upon the spirit of man.

How this salvation is obtained. I *want* to call your attention to *some* of the *elements* that are *essential*.

Man must be *willing* to be *saved*. In *order* to [do] this, he must recognize his need of salvation.

He *must* be willing to *accept* the conditions as *God* has given *them*. This seems difficult with many. [e.i.h.]

Then he *must look* to *Jesus* with an eye of *faith*. By faith, we are *justified*. It *seems* difficult to *exercise this faith*. *The just shall* live *by faith*.[188] [e.i.h.]

He *must* be willing to do *all* in *his power* for *Jesus*, working wherever he possibly *can, submitting* to the will of *God—not man—*live out the divine *requirements*.

Amen.

---

[188] Hebrews 10:38.

Sermon 13

January 30, 1898

For I determined not to know any thing among you, save Jesus Christ, and him Crucified.
—1 Corinthians 2:2

But God forbid that I should glory, save in the Cross of our Lord Jesus Christ, and him Crucified.
—Galatians 6:14

Brethren, I count not myself to have apprehended: but this one thing I do, forgetting those things which are behind, and reaching forth unto those things which are before, I press toward the mark for the prize of the high calling of God in Christ Jesus.
—Philippians 3:13–14

Many without any just cause charge *upon* our Holy *Christianity* that it necessarily begets in its followers a narrowness of intellect, equaled only by bigotry and self-imposed *slavery*. That there is no foundation for this charge in fact must appear to every mind that is candid enough to consider fairly the plan of redemption as presented to the world through Christ. [e.i.h.]

Nothing can possibly be farther from the Spirit of our Savior's teachings than bigotry, narrowness of mental vision—an inadequate provision for man's necessities or an antagonism to anything whose objective end [is] the bettering of man's Condition. And yet if we receive the teachings of certain humanitarianists (sic) as true, we must abandon the Bible view of man's real Condition—his relation as therein portrayed to his fellows and to God, and the remedy therein proposed—and look elsewhere for something to redeem man. Where shall we look? Peter said there was no one else to whom he could go save Jesus. He had the words of eternal life.

And Paul said there was no other foundation than the one already laid. Were *Jesus* to build up a system of truths, that would save humanity from *itself.*

The highest possible devotion to any Cause is the voluntary surrendering of oneself to that Cause—not to become a passive instrument but to actively engage all the powers of the soul for the accomplishment of the end in view.

This involves an intelligent conception of the cause in which we are engaged. [e.i.h.]

In Luke 16:26 and C., our Savior speaks of the kingdom of heaven with reference to this thought. There is an absolute necessity for this when we contemplate the *character* of the salvation through *Christ*. Not only with reference to the difficulties but with reference to the power of God as revealed through Christ. [e.i.h.]

There must be a willingness to use all the *means* ordained for the development of the highest possible power in the *life*. We want power with God, and we want influence with men. What will secure to us this power and *influence*?

1) To be strictly honest with *God* and with ourselves. [e.i.h.]
2) To know as much of the divine will as it is possible for us to know.
3) To act up to our convictions of duty. The limit of our convictions stops with our capacity to know.

The highest possible guarantee that can be given for the continued attachment of one to a given object is found in the fact that the mind is completely filled with the *object* around which it revolves, producing as a result a complete satisfaction. [e.i.h.]

Does this meet the requirements of our *Holy Christianity*? Or does our Holy Christianity fill the Soul? This is seen in *physical* truth. Take the philosopher—chemist—statesman—Copernicus—astronomy—Peter—Paul.

There is this *general* law that *holds good* and specially so when we come into the realm of the Spiritual. The realm of truth is so wonderful—so broad—that at each step the mind takes its mental vision is enlarged—not only to drink it in but stimulated to drink into it still deeper. *Paul* said this *one thing I do*. I *reach out* into the future. *Keep* my eye on the *end* to be obtained. [e.i.h.]

One *must* not be *trammelled* with unnecessary *difficulties*—"forgetting the things that are *behind*"—forgetting past difficulties—*past trials*, etc. Paul at Philippi.[189]

Now difficulties may encompass any *man* in *any* occupation. The *difference between* the difficulties *here and those* encompassing the *Christian. The one* amid his difficulties has nothing to comfort him but his faith in the ultimate success of his enterprise—the [other] amid his difficulties is comforted by the power of *God* through his faith in the *Lord Jesus*. [e.i.h.]

The absolute certainty of *faith* being *realized* to its *full*. Jesus says, "I go to prepare a *place* for *you*, that where I am there ye may be also."[190]

There is a surety *given* of it *here* to the believing *soul*. "Now he which stablished us with *you* in Christ, and hath anointed us in God: Who hath also sealed us and given the earnest of the Spirit in our hearts."[191]

In the text is indicated the secret of Paul's success. "For I determined not to know anything among *you* save Christ Jesus—and him *Crucified*."

Let us adopt the same if we would be successful. Amen.

---

[189] 2 Corinthians 11–23 to chapter end.
[190] John 14:3.
[191] 2 Corinthians 1:21–22.

Sermon 14

Holiness becometh thine house, O Lord, for ever.
—Psalm 93: 5

Holiness becometh thine house, O Lord, for ever. The thought that will force itself upon the mind of him who thoughtfully reads the book of Psalms will be that not only are the character and dignity of the Great *God* Presented, the relations he Sustains to the work of his hands, the Condition of man without the beneficent influence of the Spirit of God upon the heart. The happy state of mind of the righteous resting with simple faith in God blurred and run together, but of a mind fully conscious of the protective power from the arms of the Omnipotent, beneath him, and the absolute need of the heart washed and made clean, before that self-conscious realization of the action. The hand of God is felt by the individual in his own experience.

What we want to discuss is the excellency of the Christian's life and its influence upon the world. No one will question the fact that it is his imperative duty to live close to the Redeemer and that at all times he ought to maintain a godly walk and conversation. Yet some are slow to accept the fact that a pure heart or purity in the individual life is one of the imperative injunctions of the Word of God, to say nothing of the possibility of its attainment. As one has said, no earnest Christian will deny the fact but that it is his imperative duty to *be good and do good.* Whenever this sanctified Christian earnestness is found alongside of it will be found assimilated all the interest of the church of the Lord Jesus Christ.

Wherever it is wanting the work of soul saving will move on at a slow pace if not entirely clogging the wheels of salvation.

The first thought we wish to call attention to is what is the character of the holiness alluded to in the text? There has been much written and talked within the last few years concerning this idea of *Holiness*. And while there have been many who have accepted the thoughts stated, a great many have dissented, not from a spirit of bigotry, but from a conscientious conviction that in essence or in fact there was a misconception.

Some have thought that the terms used were not the most happy to convey an accurate idea of what was intended. Some have objected to the time—that perfection in its highest was attained only at the time of the dissolution of body and soul. But without stating the positions held by the many and the few concerning this doctrine, we come at once to consider its nature or character.

The only acceptable worship to God is pure, holy, without dissimulation, without hypocrisy, engaging the whole heart, divesting itself of everything selfish, low, vulgar, mean, or base.

And in speaking thus, we are not to be understood as asking for or claiming angelic perfection in the worship of God when speaking of humanity. The Bible was written for humans and not angelic beings. And as a book for us, what it contains is intended for us as such we are to interpret it. Then as such, one of the leading elements in its nature is *Consecration*.

Consecration, the generally received meaning of this word is "separation," "set apart," "to dedicate." And in the Bible, whether used with reference to individuals, or things in the worship of God, means separation, with reference to individuals, from the world to God, and of things from a secular to a sacred use. The consecration may be made up of two parts, the external and the internal, i.e., that which is in the letter which is surrounded with the formal ceremony, as in the crowning of a king, the inauguration of a president, or the consecration of a Jewish priest. *And* that in the heart where the individual solemnly affirms before God and man his faithful allegiance to the trust committed to his keeping.

It is this latter and in this last sense we believe the individual consecration of Christians is used. And it is in this sense in which it is of movement to us as Christian men and women. The conversion there is a voluntary surrender of the *will* of the individual to the *will* of *God* or in submission to God's Will. He has voluntarily relinquished the world and gives himself to the work and worship of his blessed master.

We say voluntary for there is no compulsion in the sense of force other than rewards and Jesus—inherits the love of God, the love of Jesus, the prospect of an eternal inheritance in the realm of light and the fear of death and hell and their congruent punishments on the other—to draw him away from the world and from himself and fix his heart upon God and his worship.

Here is where true Christian consecration takes place. It finds its real work done in the heart and as a necessary consequence, a corresponding influence is seen in the life. Change the heart, and the life necessarily becomes changed. You may reform the life to some extent, and the source whence are its issues still remain. Whenever and wherever in the Scriptures the corruption from sin of individuals is spoken of, it is always referred to the heart. Our Savior particularity speaks of this. That it is not what enters into a man which defiles him but what comes out from the heart: for out of the heart *proceed* evil thoughts of murder, adulteries, etc.

And the prophet speaking of the competing influences of the heart says, "The heart is deceitful above *all* things and is desperately wicked." Who can know it? The heart.

Thus, we see the consecration of the individual [to be] the result in great good to himself and the service of *God* must be in the heart. Perhaps it would be of interest to note for a short time how chiefly it was brought about. The consecration to the priest's office was a most solemn affair, as we will learn by reading the twenty-ninth chapter of Exodus. But while solemn and engaging a considerable length of time in completing the consecration, these were not more than the work demanded. And the consecration of the individual ought to be as sacred and as important when comes before *God* to consecrate himself for all time to his service, as that engaging the setting apart to a particular work. This is brought about

1) by studying to comprehend the nature of the work and the character of the being to whom and for whom we are thus dedicating ourselves, and the relations which we sustain in the matter. These three things will aid us very materially in bringing us into a proper attitude before *God*;
2) by venturing *all* upon God by simple unwavering faith in the Lord Jesus Christ. One of the chief causes perhaps of the slow progress we make in our Christian experiences is the lack of this simple implicit confidence on our part in the Lord Jesus Christ. If we could, all of us, only bring ourselves to the point where we believe without doubting, it would be a happy time in the experience and life of the individual.

But then you say possibly. How does this entire consecration affect the holiness of the individual or of the worship of *God*? Much every way to stop short of this holy Consecration to God and his service is to stop short of heaven and all its joys and pleasures. Heaven is a place of happiness and purity. The prophet says, "And an highway shall be there, and a way, and it shall be called The way of holiness; the unclean shall not pass over it; but it shall be for those: the wayfaring men, though fools, shall not err therein. No lion shall be there, nor any ravenous beast shall go up thereon, it shall not be found there; but the redeemed shall walk there: And the ransomed of the Lord shall return, and come to Zion with songs and everlasting joy upon their heads; they shall obtain joy and gladness, and sorrow and sighing shall flee away."[192]

This it seems to me expresses a condition of the individual heart. Heaven, I believe, is as much a condition as a place. The man or woman who has not the love of Jesus in the heart here has no assurance of it in the world to come. If we can't love our neighbors

---

[192] Isaiah 35:8–10.

here, have we any assurance that we can love them yonder? If malice and envy and hatred and ill will are wankling[193] in the heart? Have we any assurance that they will be removed in death? These are cast out just like everything else that stands opposed to *God's* Law, by faith in Christ and not removed through fear, and they must necessarily be done if they are removed in death.

In the completeness of the Christian's life and character, Paul says of Christians, "And ye are complete in him."[194] And again, "All Scripture is given by inspiration of God and is profitable for doctrine for reproof, for correction, for instruction in righteousness."[195] "That the man of God may be *perfect, thoroughly furnished to every good work or unto all good works.*"[196]

This completeness of the individual does not preclude the idea of growing or developing. This unfolding process is seen in nature, as the infested vitality from God gives it life and power to appropriate the elements in nature given in applying them to itself.

Apply this same idea to the child of God. This completeness is seen and realized only in Christ and in the new creation of the individual. We speak of perfect manhood and perfect womanhood without reference to the Christian character or without reference to the influence of religion on the heart. But it seems to me that this would only be a misnomer, for it certainly cannot be said of them in reference to their physical organisms, and much less could it be said in reference to their moral or spiritual natures without the influence of religion upon the heart.

If we cannot find without the influence of Christ upon the heart in charging the needed power to give humanity its proper dignity and thoroughly impart into it the proper principles, then we must turn to the world's Redeemer for the needed power.

It is indicated again in the supply. That which man does alone is more or less imperfect to a greater or lesser extent is their ignorance

---

[193] This is an unusual choice of wording. Wankle usually implies insecure or wobbly. See *Collins English Dictionary* (Twelfth edition), 2014.
[194] Colossians 2:10.
[195] 2 Timothy 3:16.
[196] 2 Timothy 3:17.

written all over it. But not so with what God does. The least of his works indicates the highest exhibition of holiness and wisdom. The wisdom and the power that create a person are as great and as perfect as that necessary to create a world. Look there at the supply to the Christian wants. That is complete since it comes from the Father of lights with whom there is no variableness, neither shadow of turning, and while what is need is *based* upon the faith of the individual. Yet the supply needed for human wants is based upon the wisdom of God. Power is imparted in conversion to the individual, giving it a vitalizing energy that confers upon the soul the image of Christ, and while this is so there is a power given from day to day that quickens and sustains the life.

Then looking at these things which indicate the completeness of the Christian's life, the necessity of these things being imparted to the individual to fit him for the duties and responsibilities of the Christian's life. And knowing the character of our *Father*, we can see why holiness becometh the house of God. May we all by the grace our heavenly Father gives to his children have the needed grace to fit us for worshiping the *great God in* sincerity, purity, and earnestness of heart. *Amen.*

Prayer added:

> Most merciful God, whose power is over all his works and whose divine providence and care extend to the least objects of thy creation, have mercy upon us as we approach thy solemn presence, and grant us, we beseech thee, thy favor and thy smiles as we attempt to worship thee. For Christ's sake, amen.

Bibliography

Allen, Tim. *A Fiery Preacher in the Old North State: A Tale from North Carolinas Oldest Church.* Raleigh, NC: www.carolinacountry, September 2016.

Andrews, Dee E. *The Methodists and Revolutionary America. 1760–1800: The Shaping of an Evangelical Culture.* Princeton, N.J.: Princeton University Press, 2002.

Arnow, Harriette Simpson. *Seedtime in the Cumberland.* New York: Macmillan, 1960.

Bardolph, Richard. "Illinois Agriculture in Transition: 1820–1870. *Journal of the Illinois State Historical Society (1908–1984).* University of Illinois Press, Vol. 41, No. 4, Dec. 1948.

Brown, George. *Recollections of Itinerant Life: Including Early Reminiscences.* Cincinnati: Carroll & Co., Publishers, 1896.

Campbell, Ted. *Methodist Church Doctrine: The Essentials.* Nashville: Abingdon Press, 2011 rev. ed.

Clark, Robert D. *The Life of Matthew Simpson.* New York: The Macmillian Company, 1956.

Clarke, Chris. "Robert Raikes and the Sunday School Movement." An Address Given to Crich Baptist Church. Crich, Derbyshire, April 25, 2015.

Crissy, Elwell. *Horse Preacher.* Tigard, Oregon: Blue Water Publishing, 1989.

Emill, Martin J. "The Illinois Central Railroad and the Development of Illinois." A thesis submitted in partial fulfillment of the requirements for the degree of Master of Arts, Loyola University, 1933.

Erwin, Rev. James. *Reminiscences of Early Circuit Life.* Toledo, Ohio: Spear, Johnson & Co., Printers, 1884.

Feinman, Peter, "Itinerant Circuit-riding Minister: Warrior of Light in a Wilderness of Chaos." *Methodist History.* 45: I, October 2006.

Ferguson, Charles W. *Methodists and the Making of America: Organizing to Beat the Devil.* Austin, Texas, Eakin Press, 1983.

Pioneer: A Narrative of the Nativity, Experience, Travels and Ministerial Labours of Rev. Charles Giles. New York: G. Lane & P.P. Sanford, 1844.

Gregory, Alfred Gregory. *Robert Raikes: Journalist and Philanthropist, a History of the Origin of Sunday-Schools.* London & Aylesbury: Hazell, Watson, & Viney, Printers Leopold Classic Library, 2015.

Harris, J. Henry Harris, Josiah Harris. *Robert Raikes, The Man and His Work.* New York: E. P. Dutton & Company, 1899.

Hattersley, Roy. *A Brand from the Burning.* London, Abacus, 2002.

Heitzenrater, Richard P. *The Elusive Mr. Wesley.* Nashville, Abingdon Press, 2003.

History of Logan County: Together with Sketches of its Cities, Villages, and Towns, Educational, Religious, Civil, Military, and Political History. Chicago: Interstate Publishing Company, 1886.

Hughes, J. Theodore. *An Historical Sketch of the Life of Freeborn Garrettson, Pioneer Methodist Preacher.* Rhinebeck, NY: Rhinebeck United Methodist Parish, 1984.

Johnson, Charles A. *The Frontier Camp: Religion's Harvest Time.* Dallas: Southern Methodist University Press, 1955.

Lincoln Herald. Lincoln, Illinois, January 26, 1871.

Outler, Albert C., and Richard P. Heitzenrater, eds. *John Wesley's Sermons, An Anthology.* Nashville: Abingdon Press, 1910.

Parker, Percy Livingstone, ed. *The Journal of John Wesley: Founder of the Methodist Movement.* N.P., F. H. Revell, 2016.

Richey, Russell E. *Methodism in the American Forest.* New York: Oxford University Press, 2015.

Ruth, Lester. *A Little Heaven Below: Worship at Early Methodist Quarterly Meetings.* Nashille: Kingswood Books, 2000.

Salaman, Sonya. *Prairie Patrimony, Family, Farming in the Midwest.* Chapel Hill: University of North Carolina Press, 1955.

Sawicki, Marianne. *The Gospel in History: Portrait of a Teaching Church; The Origins of Christian Education.* New York: Paulist Press, 1988.

Schisler, John Q. *Christian Education in Local Methodist Churches.* Nashville and New York: Abingdon Press, 1969.

Seymour, Jack L. *From Sunday School to Church School: Continuities in Protestant Education in the United States, 1869–1929.* Washington, DC: University Press of America, Inc., 1982.

Smith, Henry. *Recollections and Reflections of an Old Itinerant: Letters of Rev. Henry Smith.* Annotated by Daniel E. Garrett. 2014 Revised Edition by Daniel E. Garrett.

Stevens, Abel. *History of the Methodist Episcopal Church in the United States of America.* New York: Eaton and Mains, 1900.

Stone, Phillip. *How the Methodist Church Split in the 1840s.* Blog: wofford.edu, 2013.

Stover, John. "The Illinois Central Railroad and the Growth of Illinois and Chicago in the 1850s." *Railway History*, Autumn 1988, No. 159.

The Methodist Church. *Recent Membership Trends.* True Discipleship, 2020.

The Moody Church History Timeline, *The Clapham Group.* Christianity.com, Salem Web Network, 2016.

The Radio Times

Wigger, John H. *Taking Heaven by Storm: Methodism and the Rise of Popular Christianity in America.* Urbana and Chicago: University of Illinois Press, 2001.

Winslow, Hubbard. *Elements of Moral Philosophy.* New York: D. Appleton and Company, 1856.

About the Author

Sharon Grimes Knox is a graduate of Westminster Choir College, Princeton, New Jersey (1964) with a degree in voice and organ. In 1977, she enrolled in Duke University, Durham, North Carolina, as a graduate student in the department of history, obtaining a master's degree in 1979 and a PhD in 1986. She remained at Duke where she taught Western European History and was an assistant director of the Duke Pre-major Advising Center. Singing in the Duke chapel choir, the group sang extensively, spreading the Gospel in China, Russia, the Czech Republic, Italy, and England. In 1991, she was awarded the Duke University Alumni Association's Distinguished Undergraduate Teaching Award.

Dr. Knox's publication of *The British National Health Service: State Intervention in the Medical Marketplace, 1911–1948* was published by Garland, Publishing, Inc. in 1991 under the name Sharon Schildein Grimes. It was reissued by Routledge in 2017 as part of its library editions, the History of Social Welfare.

In retirement, Dr. Knox keeps busy in her adopted home in Furry Creek, British Columbia. She is active in community organizations and is a member of St. John the Divine Anglican Church.

Dr. Knox has two sons, six stepchildren, thirteen grandchildren, and two great-grandchildren. She was predeceased by her husbands John Harlin Grimes, MD and James Henry Knox.

CPSIA information can be obtained
at www.ICGtesting.com
Printed in the USA
BVHW031446091121
621076BV00026B/289